D1288770

PSYCHOLOGY FOR KIDS

The Science of the Mind and Behavior

Books for Kids from the
American Psychological Association.

Book design by Collaborate Agency, Ltd.
Printed by Worzalla, Stevens Point, WI

Library of Congress Cataloging-in-Publication Data
Names: Toner, Jacqueline B., author. | Freeland, Claire A. B., author.
Title: Psychology for kids : the science of the mind and behavior
by Jacqueline B. Toner, PhD and Claire A. B. Freeland, PhD.
Description: [Washington] : Magination Press, [2021] | Includes index. |
Summary: "This introduction to the science of psychology for young readers features chapters on the brain, personality, intelligence, emotions, social relationships, and more"— Provided by publisher.
Identifiers: LCCN 2020044360 (print) | LCCN 2020044361 (ebook) |: ISBN 9781433832109 (hardback) | ISBN 9781433836923 (ebook)
Subjects: LCSH: Psychology—Juvenile literature.
Classification: LCC BF149.5 .T66 2021 (print) | LCC BF149.5 (ebook) | DDC 155.4—dc23
LC record available at https://lccn.loc.gov/2020044360
LC ebook record available at https://lccn.loc.gov/2020044361

PSYCHOLOGY FOR KIDS

The Science of the Mind and Behavior

by Jacqueline B. Toner, PhD, and Claire A. B. Freeland, PhD

Magination Press • Washington, DC
American Psychological Association

To Kaitlin Toner Raimi,
PhD, with love and
thanks for her support
in this endeavor—JBT

To my parents, Lawrence and
Devora Bennett, who nurtured
my love of learning and
science—CABF

Contents

Part 1: Exploring Psychology

Chapter 1 What Is Psychology? 8

Chapter 2 Where's the Proof? 16

Part 2: Mind and Body Working Together

Chapter 3 Is Putting On Your Socks a Superpower? 26

Chapter 4 How Does the Brain Work? 36

Part 3: The One and Only Me

Chapter 5 What Makes Me "Me"? 50

Chapter 6 What Does It Mean to Be a Boy or a Girl? 62

Part 4: Learning and Growing

Chapter 7 How Did You Learn That? 74

Chapter 8 What Does It Mean to Be Smart? 84

Chapter 9 How Do You Remember? 96

Chapter 10 How Do We Think? 106

Chapter 11 How Do You Change As You Grow? 116

Part 5: Understanding Feelings

Chapter 12 How Do You Feel? 128

Chapter 13 What Motivates You? 138

Part 6: Caring for Yourself

Chapter 14 What Is Stress? 150

Chapter 15 Why Do You Spend So Much Time Sleeping? 160

Part 7: Taming Emotions

Chapter 16 What Helps People Do Well? 170

Chapter 17 What About When It All Feels Like Too Much? 180

Part 8: Living With Others

Chapter 18 Why Are Other People So Important? 192

Chapter 19 How Can You Understand Other People's Experiences? 202

Chapter 20 Is Conflict Part of Being Human? 212

Part 9: Planning for a Better World

Chapter 21 Can Psychology Help Save Planet Earth? 224

Glossary 234

Index 248

About the Authors 256

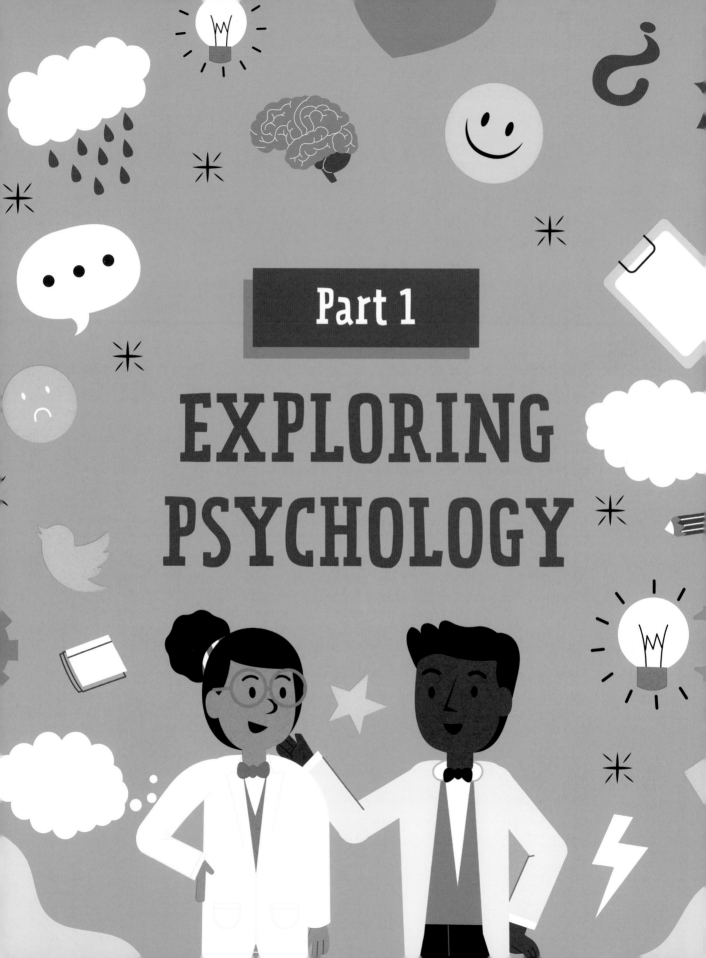

Part 1

EXPLORING PSYCHOLOGY

Chapter 1

WHAT IS PSYCHOLOGY?

Why do optical illusions trick us? Do other people feel and think the same way you do? Can animals be taught language? Why do you sleep? You can explore these questions (and many others) through the fascinating science of psychology.

What exactly is psychology? One common definition describes psychology as "the science of the mind and behavior." In your **mind**, you experience emotions, thoughts, and the reasons for doing what you do—these are actions that other people can't see. **Behavior** is how a person (or animal) acts. Behaviors are actions that other people can see, such as recycling, doing homework, exercising, talking, and making faces.. Psychologists are interested in how the mind powers behaviors and how behaviors relate to the world around you.

WHAT DO PSYCHOLOGISTS DO?

You might already know what some psychologists do. School psychologists, for example, evaluate students who are having any sort of difficulty at school, such as problems with learning or behavior. But there are lots of other kinds of psychologists, some who do research, and some who apply research findings in different settings. Let's learn about the work of a few real-life psychologists.

Dr. Tim Nichols studied how people use video games. For example, when you fail at a video game, what makes you try again? "I am passionate about understanding technology's role in satisfying fundamental human needs like connecting with others, personal growth, escapism, and showing off pictures of their dogs. I like figuring out why people do what they do, and I love building great teams of smart researchers who are passionate about the same. When I tell people I work in video games and that I have a doctorate in research psychology, they usually wait for the punch line."

Dr. Johan Lundström's research looked at how people responded to smells. Is that smelly cheese or vomit? If you are blindfolded when you take a sniff, your answer will depend on what you're told. Your sense of smell depends on what you know and what you think!

Dr. Kathleen Kremer worked with toy designers, taking research results and using them to make toys kids would love. "You need to know their wants, needs, abilities, constraints and behaviors. You then use this information to figure out what to make and how to make it."

Dr. Susan Clayton studied how people connect with animals and nature, and how those connections might lead them to conserve our natural resources. "In my research at zoos, I found that almost nine out of ten visitors will share their observations of an animal by pointing it out to their companions, or simply by saying 'look!' Social interactions like these are opportunities to create and communicate shared values."

Dr. Jennifer Manly studied how good quality early childhood education may protect the brain from disorders related to aging.

Her research showed, for example, that people who had brain disorders when they were old had gone to schools that spent less money on their students each year and had shorter school years.

Dr. Manly's work influenced other researchers to consider the quality of people's education as important to their physical or medical condition throughout their lives.

You can learn more about these and other psychologists on the American Psychological Association website! Psychologists like these are a curious bunch, and their quest to understand the confusing, surprising, and sometimes silly world of the human mind and behavior takes them along many different paths. Some study how we take in information and make sense of it. Others try to understand how we learn and when that learning sticks (and when it doesn't). Still others are interested in how people interact and influence each other. The list goes on!

Try This

Take a look at these questions. Four are real questions psychologists are working to answer. One isn't.

1. What's the best way to convince people to protect the environment?

2. Can you tell if someone is lying by watching their face?

3. What fire truck color is the safest?

4. How quickly is the universe expanding?

5. Will people see someone in a gorilla suit if they walk right through a ball game?

Number four is a question psychologists are not working on. Psychologists don't study the expansion of the universe—physicists have that covered. But they do study the other questions and many more...

WHAT DO PSYCHOLOGISTS STUDY?

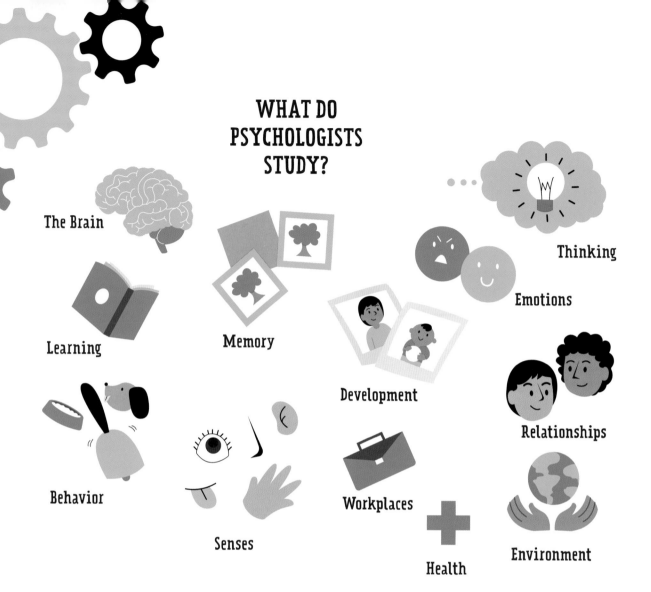

The Brain

Learning

Memory

Development

Thinking

Emotions

Relationships

Behavior

Senses

Workplaces

Health

Environment

HOW DO PSYCHOLOGISTS ANSWER QUESTIONS?

Say you want to encourage people to change their behavior in ways that help the environment. You can probably think of some ideas such as these:

- Send an email to all the families in my school about the importance of recycling.

- Give each family in my neighborhood a cloth bag for groceries so they don't use plastic.

- Set up a booth at a local fair to provide information about setting the thermostat in homes to use less energy.

These all sound like good ideas, but how can you find out which ones actually work? A **research psychologist** uses science to gather evidence to see if what people think will work actually does.

We all have ideas about why things are the way they are. You might have a very strong opinion that you study better with music playing in the background. But a psychologist would actually gather data about how kids did after studying with music compared to those who studied in quiet. They would probably even check whether it makes a difference if the music has words or not. The difference between opinion and science is evidence!

Check Out the Research

Let's look at one question that psychologists tried to answer:

How can we get hotel guests to reuse their towels?

Why is this important? Well, hotels use a lot of water and energy washing guests' towels every day. It would help the environment if guests would agree to hang up and reuse their towels. Maybe putting a sign in the bathroom asking them to do just that would be a good idea. But psychologists didn't just guess what might work: they tested to see whether it did.

Help save the environment
Most guests reuse towels

Join your fellow guests in helping to save the environment. Three out of four guests reuse their towels during their stay!

So did a sign work? Research in 2008 by psychologists Noah Goldstein, Robert Cialdini, and Vladas Griskevicius showed that it did, but the words on the sign mattered too! The psychologists found that if people were told that reusing their towels would help the environment, some people did reuse them. But if they told people that *most* visitors to the hotel chose to reuse towels, a lot more people decided to do so. That suggested that people are encouraged to do what they believe other people are doing.

WHAT DO PSYCHOLOGISTS DO WITH THEIR DISCOVERIES?

While it's cool to study the answers to interesting questions, psychologists also want that information to be used to solve problems or make people's lives better. When psychologists use information learned from research studies to solve a problem, we call it **applied psychology**. In addition to telling hotels how to word their signs so that guests reuse their towels, psychological studies have shown us many different ways to improve our lives and our society.

- Psychologists consult with businesses to improve efficiency, cut down on absences, and increase worker satisfaction.

- Psychological research has shown that people may not remember what they've seen as well as they think they do; this has made people re-evaluate eyewitness reports of crimes.

- Psychologists have used research on people's health-related behaviors to give effective advice on how best to change bad habits.

- Psychologists have looked at how screen time affects learning and brain development, and have advised parents to strictly limit screen time with young children.

Companies, government agencies, universities, sports teams, and hospitals all rely on psychologists to perform and apply research. Chances are, you are benefitting from the work of psychologists every day. This book will show you a lot more about how psychologists work, what they know, and how that work is improving lives.

NOW YOU KNOW!

- Psychology is the science of behavior and the mind.

- Psychologists work in many different settings and study many different questions.

- Research psychologists search for evidence to answer questions.

- Research findings are often used to help people or society make positive changes. This is called applied psychology.

Chapter 2
WHERE'S THE PROOF?

Like all sciences, psychology relies on research to provide evidence about how to solve some of society's challenges. While psychologists don't use lasers, telescopes, or trowels, the rules they follow to answer questions are the same ones used for scientific research in physics, astronomy, or paleontology. Just like researchers in those fields, psychologists make observations and develop theories and **hypotheses**. Hypotheses are the scientist's best guess about how an experiment will turn out. Then they collect **data** to test them. If you want to know more about how those **experiments** work, understand what they can (and can't) tell us, or design a psychology experiment of your own, read on!

WHAT MAKES PSYCHOLOGY A SCIENCE?

Psychologists use the **scientific method** to answer questions they are interested in. This means they follow these steps when doing research:

1. Make some observations.
2. Narrow down a question.
3. Form a hypothesis.
4. Design an experiment and collect data.
5. Decide whether the data from the experiment supports the hypothesis.

SCIENCE ON THE PLAYGROUND

Here's an example of how you might use the scientific method in practice. Since you've had years of experience on playgrounds, you and some classmates are asked to consult on how to improve the playground at a local elementary school. Let's apply the scientific method to your assignment.

1. First, make some observations of the playground. You might make a list of each piece of playground equipment and notice how it's being used: for example, maybe there's a line for the swings.
2. Narrow down a question to study: Do we need more swings?
3. Form a hypothesis: There aren't enough swings.
4. Design a study and collect data. You could keep count of each time a kid used the swings, how long kids were waiting to use a swing, and how long each kid stayed on the swings. Later you could compare those counts.

5. If kids tended to stay a long time on the swings and other kids didn't get turns, the study would show that the hypothesis was correct: there aren't enough swings. If no one had to wait a long time, and everybody had a turn, the hypothesis was *not* supported: there are enough swings.

This study would give information about how kids use the swings on the playground. A next step experiment might look at how children react when a line has formed to wait for swings. For example, you could place three, five, and seven children in each of three lines and see if kids coming over to use a swing will only wait if the line is short. How children use playground equipment is one example of helpful psychology research. There may be other ideas about how to improve the playground. Perhaps the next study could look at how kids feel about the playground. To find out the children's opinions, you could **survey** every kid in the school about which piece of equipment they like best, what they usually do on the playground, and what they think would make the playground better. A survey asks individuals questions about a subject.

Of course, you'd need to be sure to ask all of the kids, not just a few. Or, if there are too many kids to ask everyone, you would want to be sure to ask a **sample** that includes different kinds of kids (for example, girls and boys, younger kids and older kids) so that the opinions of the sample are more likely to match those of the whole group. A survey is a useful way of learning about what groups of people think and feel. And a project that uses a survey will follow the scientific method.

WHICH COMES FIRST, YOUTUBE OR GRADES?

Careful experiments can help you figure out what truly causes something. That's not always straightforward! What if someone noticed that kids who watch a lot of YouTube videos do poorly in school? Does watching YouTubes cause poor grades? Not necessarily: maybe kids with poor grades watch more YouTube. Or maybe neither is true: something else causes poor grades and a lot of YouTube watching.

When we notice two things tend to happen together, this is called a **correlation**. We may think that if things go together, one thing led to another, like in the YouTube example. However, it might have just been a coincidence, the cause could have been reversed, or the cause for both may be something entirely different. Studying **causation**, or how one thing causes another, is more complicated and requires doing an experiment.

One way to answer questions about causation is to compare a **sample group** that the psychologist does something to (say, doesn't allow them to watch YouTube for a month) to a similar group (**control group**) that doesn't get that treatment (no limits on YouTube time) to see if it makes a difference (in grades). Or you can compare the same people to themselves under different conditions (no YouTube for a month versus no limits on YouTube for another month).

Experiments with a sample group and a control group help to narrow down possible explanations for behaviors. When experiments build on one another, we get more and more confident that we know the cause for a particular behavior.

CHECK YOUR WORK!

Even careful researchers can't plan for all the elements that can influence their scientific results in unexpected ways. Research findings can be misleading if a study suffers from **sampling bias.** If there are too few people (or animals) in a sample, the findings are less likely to be true in general. If the sample only includes one group of people, research findings might not apply to other groups.

Scientific papers explain their research designs carefully so that other psychologists can try the same experiment. If a study can't be repeated with similar results, it suggests that unplanned factors influenced the results.

Most research focuses on what happens during the time of a study. But we often want to know if the effects will last. To really explore that question requires a **longitudinal** study, where you follow people over months, years, or even decades.

Even when a study is designed well, the interpretation of the findings can be limited. Later research may show that other explanations for the results also make sense. This is why psychologists talk about evidence *supporting* a hypothesis rather than *proving* it. It's always possible that later research may reveal a different explanation for a study's findings.

Check Out the Research

In the 1960s and 1970s Walter Mischel and his team did a very famous experiment called the "Marshmallow Test." They put one preschooler at a time at a table with a marshmallow in front of them. Then the experimenter said they needed to leave for a bit and gave the child the choice of eating that one marshmallow while they were gone or, if they could wait, they'd give them two later. Some of the kids went ahead and ate the marshmallow. But others worked hard to resist. They hid their eyes so they couldn't see it. They squirmed in their seats. But they waited and got the bigger treat.

Search "Marshmallow Test" on the internet to see examples of how the study was set up.

In this longitudinal study, the researchers looked at how life turned out for the kids many years later and were amazed to learn that kids who could wait for the bigger treat were more successful in school, healthier, and even had differences in their brains years later! Those were pretty amazing findings, but did they actually prove that you can tell how well someone will do as an adult based on whether they can wait for a treat when they're little? Well, it seems it's not that simple.

Recently, another group of researchers tried the same study and didn't find the same results. They used a bigger sample of kids, a sample with less sampling bias.

While the initial sample was a small group of kids from well-off families, this second sample included kids with more differences in how much money their families had and whether their parents had gone to college. It turned out that success later in life was more related to the advantages a kid had at home than whether or not they could wait for a larger treat.

Walter Mischel's team did lots of different studies looking at children's self-control and many of their findings were useful then and now. However, we now know that families have a big influence over how their children develop.

Explore Further

SPECIAL RESEARCH PARTICIPANTS

Psychological studies sometimes use animals as participants. They are particularly helpful when the researcher needs to have more control over the participants' experiences than is possible with people. You'll read in Chapter 7 how a psychologist named B.F. Skinner used animals to study learning. He was able to do his research because he could carefully control his animal participants' food and environment.

Identical twins are another very interesting group to include in research. Psychologists often want to study whether people act or experience things the way they do because of inborn differences or because of their environment and life experiences. This is referred to as **"nature versus nurture."** Identical twins inherit the same genes from both of their parents, so when twins show different behaviors, feelings, or thoughts, it's probably due to what they learned through life experience.

Studies of identical twins who were separated as infants and adopted into very different circumstances sometimes found similarities in behavior and preferences later in life. In one example, Oskar and Jack, identical twins adopted by different families and raised in different countries far apart, were similar in surprising ways as adults. Both thought it was funny to sneeze in crowded places. Both flushed the toilet before they used it. Both read magazines from back to front. And both liked to dip their buttered toast in coffee.

RESEARCH SHOULDN'T HURT

As you read about the research of early psychologists, you may feel upset about how some studies were unpleasant or harmful to their animal or human participants. While these studies led to important findings, psychologists today wouldn't think it was okay. In fact, modern psychologists need to explain to others how their experiments are **ethical**. Human volunteers need to be told that they are in an experiment and agree to participate. If anything could hurt or upset them, they need to be warned, and if they are hurt in any way, they need to be provided with help. There are also careful protections for animals in research.

Try This

Ready to try your own psychology experiment? Use the example below as a guide.

Hypothesis: Kids perform better on spelling tests when they review the words an hour before the test.

Participants: Two groups of kids: the experimental group has an extra review an hour before the test. The control group does not get the experimental treatment—they get the usual spelling test.

Test the hypothesis: Compare the test grades of the two groups.

Examine the data: Decide whether the data supports the hypothesis and describe exactly how the study was done in enough detail that another researcher would be able repeat it.

(Of course, because we want to be ethical researchers, if we really did this study, we would ask for permission from parents to have their children participate.)

Your turn. Can you think of a question you would like to answer? Can you design a research study to learn more about it? If you don't have any ideas right now, read ahead to learn what kinds of research psychologists have done. Then come back and see what interesting experiments you can design.

NOW YOU KNOW!

○ Just like other sciences, psychology uses the scientific method to answer research questions. A research psychologist comes up with a hypothesis, or best guess, about the answer to their question and then carefully collects data to test it.

○ A psychologist may observe whether research participants behave the way their hypothesis predicts they will. Or, a psychologist may conduct a survey and ask participants what they think or how they feel about something.

○ If a psychologist finds that two things go together (correlation) they can't say that one made the other happen (causation). Researching causation requires comparing the effect of an experimental treatment on a sample group to the effect on a control group who doesn't get the experimental treatment.

○ Each psychology research project is one piece in a very large puzzle of understanding behavior and the mind.

○ Some early psychology research couldn't be done today because it caused or threatened harm to participants. Today's psychologists take great care to make sure that their research is ethical.

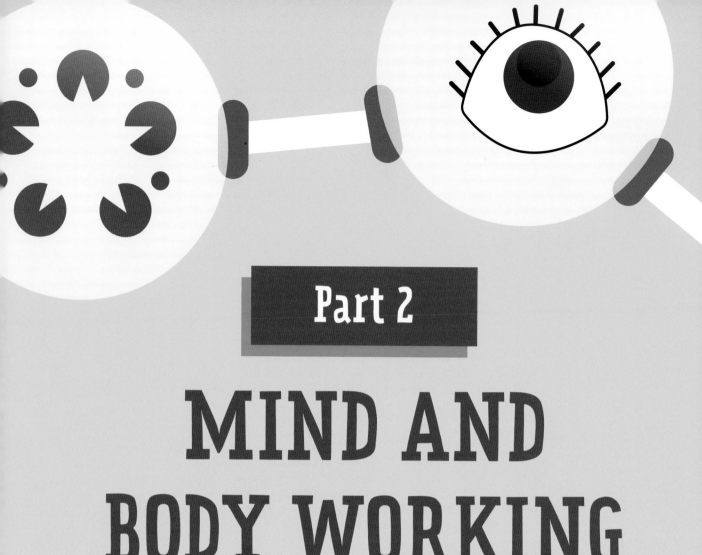

Part 2

MIND AND BODY WORKING TOGETHER

Chapter 3

IS PUTTING ON YOUR SOCKS A SUPERPOWER?

Think about one of the simple things you do every day, like putting on your socks. While it seems very easy, putting on socks needs your mind and body to work together in surprisingly complex ways. First, you need to locate your socks. Then you have to locate your feet: You need to see them and have a sense of where they are in space. And then you need your feet and hands to work together to get those socks on your feet. Putting on your socks may not be a true superpower, but it's a skill that animals don't have.

Many daily tasks depend on combining and organizing the information from your **senses**. Senses pick up information from the physical world. But your perception of the world is not just about what your senses tell you. How they are interpreted depends on past experiences and expectations. Psychologists are interested in how people make those interpretations.

WHEN IN DOUBT, BRAINS MAKE STUFF UP!

The human brain likes things to be organized and complete. It likes it so much that it will use whatever information it can to put together a neat whole.

While we all talk about our eyes seeing, eyes only do part of the job. The information gathered from your eyes travels to your brain to be understood. Your brain uses your past experience of the world to make sense of information provided by your eyes. Sometimes what your brain perceives isn't totally accurate, like when you look at optical illusions.

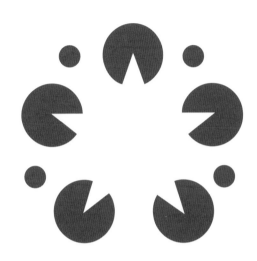

Look at the picture to the right. What is in the center?

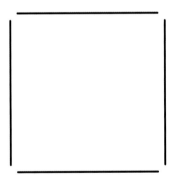

Most people see a star, but stop for a minute: how many points does the star have? Do you "see" five? Do you see 10? Are there points between the circles or just points over the circles? Is there really a star at all, or just five circles with a pie shape cut out of each? Why do most people see a star that isn't really there? Your eyes don't really sense a star, but your brain tries to interpret information from your eyes in a way that you easily understand. So, the brain fills in the gap with the idea of a "star," which can help you process what you're looking at.

In the same way, the image above and to the left is understood by the brain to be a square, even though it's missing its four corners and is really only four separate lines. Your brain interprets the picture to the left as a complete person, even though the hips and legs aren't included.

Try to read this aloud:

Our brns can stll rd wrds evn if vwls r mssng. We r abl to fll in the gps.

Were you able to read that? Amazing, huh?

DO YOU SEE WHAT I SEE?

Have you ever looked at clouds and started to see familiar objects in them? Or stared for a long time at a tiled ceiling, kitchen counter, or cracks in a sidewalk and seen designs? If so, you're not alone. Your brain is taking in what your eyes see and trying to make sense of it by fitting it into a sensible pattern, one you've seen before.

Try This

Ask friends and family to read this out loud as fast as they can.

$$8, 9, 10, 11, 12, B, 14, 15, 16$$

Does anyone read the "B" as 13? Why would that happen?

Your brain doesn't just look for visual patterns. Did you ever hear someone say that wearing your PJs inside out will ensure a snow day? Or that Friday the 13th is bad luck? Superstitions like these occur when your brain tries to tie different things together—even if they don't really belong together. This tendency to see patterns in random associations is called **apophenia**.

EXPERIENCE INFLUENCES OUR PERCEPTIONS

Some optical puzzles confuse our brains by not following the rules we've learned about how the world works. Even though this elephant has an extra leg, most people rely on their knowledge that elephants only have four legs, and may not notice the extra one. Their brains make an assumption based on experience.

An artist named M.C. Escher loved to make drawings that confuse the brain's ability to "see" clearly. Look him up in the library or online to see some examples.

People from different cultures have different experiences, and so, may perceive the world in different ways.

Most American children and adults would see a hunter about to spear an antelope with an elephant in the distance. But a researcher named William Hudson studying groups in several parts of Africa discovered that they found this picture very confusing. Many of them (kids and adults) thought the man was hunting a tiny elephant. They perceived that he must be hunting the elephant because it was closer on the page to him. They didn't perceive the elephant as being far off in the distance.

Why would people from different places perceive pictures differently? Prior experiences with art may explain it. In American culture we have learned that, in pictures, when things are smaller and higher up, that's showing that they are farther away. The experiences our brains have had with that way of showing distance in a flat drawing changes how we perceive pictures. Artists use our brains' experiences to help their pictures communicate distance. However, in other cultures, artists may use different methods to communicate distance, so people might make different assumptions when looking at an image.

THE IMPORTANCE OF TOUCH

Touch is another important sense. Early psychologists thought that babies learned to trust and cling to their mothers because their mothers were the ones who fed them. Researcher Harry Harlow wasn't so sure. He thought a mother's touch was important.

To answer the question, Harlow took two groups of baby monkeys away from their mothers. Each was given two artificial "moms"—one made of wire and another that was soft and cuddly. For one group of baby monkeys, the cuddly mom doll also had a bottle that fed them. For the other group, the wire mom fed them.

If food was the important way that babies learned to love their moms, we would expect that both groups would want to spend time with the mom with the bottle, whether it was soft or made of wire. But, surprise! All the monkeys liked to spend time with the cuddly, soft mom doll, whether that was where they got food or not. And if they were startled or afraid, it was cuddly mom they all ran to in order to feel safe. It seems that the feeling of softness was perceived by the babies as a sign that these "mothers" would care for and protect them.

YOUR EARS DO MORE THAN HEAR

Another important sense is hearing. Your amazing ears collect vibrations in the air and send them to a membrane that increases the intensity of those vibrations. The vibrations are then transferred to little hairs, which tickle nerves that send messages to your brain about the vibrations, and your brain interprets them as sound. If different information is coming to each ear through headphones, your clever brain can put the information together, or can choose to listen to one message while ignoring another.

And, hearing is not the only sensation that comes from your ears. Deep in your ear, there are canals of fluid that work with gravity to help your brain locate your body in space. In other words, they tell you about your balance. Hair fibers within these canals provide the brain with information about how that fluid is moving, which helps you perceive whether you are right side up or upside down or spinning around.

Which way is up?

YOUR SENSES OFTEN WORK TOGETHER

You may have noticed that the way something looks may influence your other senses. If something looks icky, you may expect that it won't feel nice and be quick to pull away. If a flower is pretty, you may expect it to smell nice and it may seem even worse if it unexpectedly smells bad. In their effort to work together to understand something, your senses can get fooled or confused.

Have someone cross their wrists, put their palms facing one another, and intertwine their fingers. Next, ask them to turn their clasped hands down and around towards their body and then up.

Without touching them, point to one of their fingers and ask them to move it. Does it take them a minute to find the right finger to move? Try with another finger. Now, touch one of their fingers and notice how much easier it is for them to identify and move the finger. Why?

Well, when you changed their hands so their fingers were in a very unfamiliar position, the information from their eyes got confused. By touching their fingers, another sensory system gave them additional information, which made locating each finger much easier.

A small number of people have surprising sensory experiences. When one sense is stimulated, it triggers another sense. This is called **synesthesia**. For example, someone who has synesthesia may see certain colors when they hear certain sounds or words. Or they may associate numbers with certain locations in space.

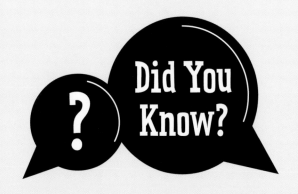

While all your senses can combine in a variety of ways to help your brain understand the world, taste and smell work especially closely together. Because of this, you may find that things don't taste the same if your nose is stuffy from a cold. For people with certain medical conditions that interfere with their sense of smell, food can have weird flavors or not much flavor at all.

Your taste buds detect five types of taste—salty, bitter, sour, umami (meaty), and sweet—and send that information to your brain. At the same time, your sense of smell adds more information. This information is combined so your brain can perceive flavor. Without being able to smell, it can be hard to know what you are eating. Here's an experiment to try with a helper.

- Get a small, peeled piece of raw potato and a small, peeled piece of apple. Don't let your helper see the pieces unless their size and shape are exactly alike. Or, if you are the participant, have your helper hide them from you.

- Blindfold the participant and have them hold their nose closed the entire time they taste the potato or apple.

- Ask them to guess if it was a potato or an apple.

- Repeat with the other piece of food.

- A piece of onion would also taste the same, but the different texture would give it away.

You can also try comparing chocolate and vanilla ice cream or pudding. Your participant may be able to tell that they are both sweet, but not which flavor of sweet.

NOW YOU KNOW!

○ You have five senses: sight, hearing, taste, smell, and touch.

○ Your senses take in information from the world and communicate with your brain about what's out there. Your brain then interprets that information. This is called perception.

○ Your brain has certain expectations about the world based upon your experiences and the brain's preference for things to fit into patterns. When the world doesn't fit into those expectations, your brain can get fooled.

○ In addition to hearing, your ears also help you to keep track of where you are in space.

○ Your senses work together to create the perception of flavor.

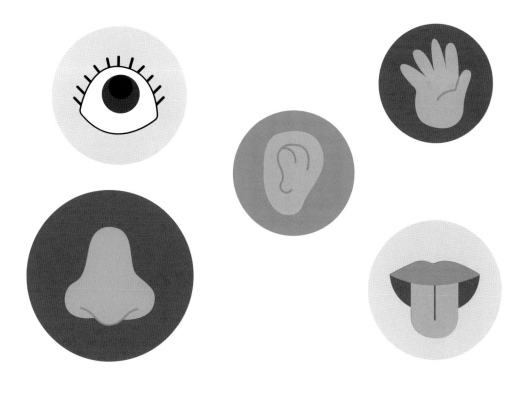

Chapter 4

HOW DOES THE BRAIN WORK?

Your brain is the most amazing organ in your body! Just about three pounds by the time you are an adult, this squishy, wrinkled blob keeps your body going and makes you you. Psychologists are interested in how the brain develops and controls thoughts, emotions, personality, memory, language, and behavior. How does the brain send messages and receive feedback? What do the different parts of the brain do? The science of the mind starts with the brain.

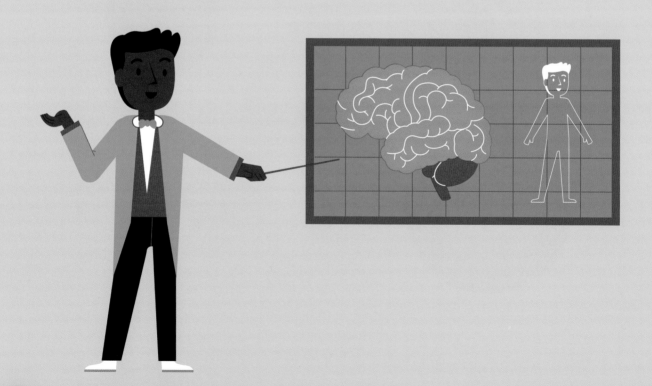

BRAIN PARTS

You can think of the brain as being divided up in a number of ways. It has two halves that are called the right and left brain **hemispheres**. You can also think about going deeper and deeper into the brain. The **cerebral cortex** is the largest part of the brain and is where perception, language, speech, learning, and controlling movements happens. Underneath that is the **cerebellum**, which keeps us upright, and helps us stay balanced. Deeper still is the **brainstem**. It houses nerve connections from other parts of the brain to the spinal cord so messages can be sent to control breathing, movement, heart rate, and wake and sleep cycles.

The cerebral cortex (that big surrounding part of the brain) can also be divided into four parts: **frontal lobe, temporal lobe, parietal lobe,** and **occipital lobe**. You'll see in this chapter how those lobes can be further divided into areas that are especially important to certain functions.

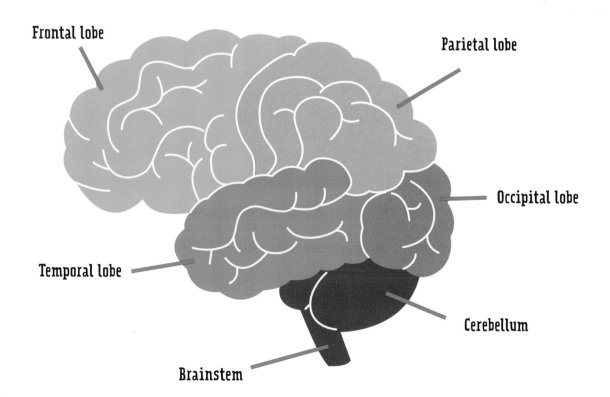

Frontal lobe

Parietal lobe

Occipital lobe

Temporal lobe

Cerebellum

Brainstem

BRAIN ACTIVITY

One of the most exciting findings in brain research is that the brain can change, a process called **neuroplasticity**. In order to understand how this happens, you need to know something about the nervous system. The nervous system is a web of cells that sends messages from the brain to the body and from the body to the brain. It is an information highway that controls everything that you do, from breathing to walking to thinking and feeling. Messages are sent by nerve cells, known as **neurons**. Neurons send signals from one to another with the help of brain chemicals. In recent years, researchers have realized that the information highway can be re-routed, resulting in changes in nervous system activity. Here's where psychologists get really interested. It's pretty cool to think that a person might be able to make changes to their brain through changes in behavior.

Psychologists and other scientists use ways of measuring the brain to show brain—behavior relationships. The technology for brain imaging is incredible. Here are a few ways to see a living brain. In each of these technologies, typically a person is laying down and is then put through a machine that records their brain activity. A computer program analyzes the data, allowing researchers to look in depth at different parts of the brain.

PROCEDURE	WHAT IT DOES
Computed Tomography (CT) Scan	Uses special x-rays taken from many different angles, which the computer puts together. It's like looking at a slice of bread from a loaf—except it's a slice of brain!
Positron Emission Tomography (PET) Scan	Uses a special dye that is absorbed by active areas of the brain. The computer can then show researchers what parts of the brain are busy working under which circumstances by showing where the dye is absorbed.
Magnetic Resonance Imaging (MRI)	Uses powerful magnets and radio waves and a computer to make detailed pictures of the brain.
Functional magnetic resonance imaging (fMRI)	Detects changes in blood flow to particular areas of the brain to show which brain areas are involved in different behaviors.

Check Out the Research

You know that you can learn and get better at all sorts of things. But brain measurement technology lets researchers actually see the changes in the brain that happen as you learn! Teresa Iuculano, with a team of researchers, identified a group of children who were having particular trouble learning math and also a group without a math learning problem. They then had the children do math during fMRIs. They could see differences in the brains of the kids with and without math learning problems. After eight weeks of math tutoring, they did fMRIs again to look for changes in the neuron connections in the brain and to compare the kids' brains again. And after tutoring, there were brain changes—so that the students who had trouble with math now resembled the students who had been better at math in brain activity AND in actually doing math! That's neuroplasticity!

You can experience your brain in action by measuring how fast you react. There are simple **reaction time** tests you can take online. Find out how long it takes your brain to see an image and click. Your neurons are sending messages from your brain to your eyes, back to your brain, and to your hand amazingly quickly.

TWO HALVES MAKE A WHOLE BRAIN

The cerebral cortex, the outer part of the brain, sets people apart from other species. Some animals have larger brains overall, but humans have the largest and most complex cerebral cortex, where thinking, planning, reasoning, language, and judgment take place. The cerebral cortex is divided into two halves, known as hemispheres. The hemispheres are connected by nerve cells so that the two parts of the brain can communicate. The left hemisphere takes the lead for language and speech and the right hemisphere specializes in spatial and pattern recognition. But people aren't left-brained or right-brained. The whole brain works together: the left side of the brain talks to the right side of the body and the right talks to the left.

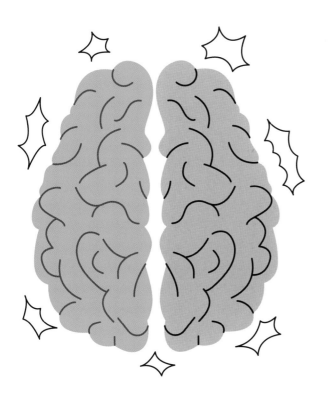

Most people are right-handed, which means the nerve pathways from the left side of the brain are stronger for using the right hand. But surprise! Most left-handed people also have stronger nerve pathways from the left side of the brain. And, your preferred foot, ear, and eye may differ from your preferred hand. Scientists still don't completely understand this sidedness business. There are brain mysteries yet to solve!

Try This

It is easy to find out someone's preferred hand—just ask them to write their name. You can test their preferred foot by putting a coin on the floor in front of them and asking them to step on it (you can also look at what foot they begin with to walk the stairs or what foot they use to kick a ball). Ask them to look through a paper towel cardboard tube to find out which eye they prefer—whichever eye they automatically hold it up to is probably it. To determine which ear is preferred, tell them you are going to whisper in their ear and see which one they turn towards you. Were you able to find someone who was right-handed but left-eyed, eared, or footed? How about someone who prefers their left everything consistently? Take your sidedness research a step further and try using your less preferred hand, foot, eye, and ear to perform activities for a period of time. How big a difference does this make?

MORE ABOUT THE PARTS OF THE BRAIN

You now know that the brain has two hemispheres. Let's look within each hemisphere to understand some of the parts within the brain. The frontal lobes are headquarters for thought, attention, problem solving, planning, and judgment. Toward the back of the frontal lobes, the **motor cortex** controls voluntary movement, like moving your arms and legs. The parietal lobes, which sit behind the frontal lobes, help with putting together information about your senses and help you know where you are in space. Bite into a slice of pizza and your parietal lobes are checking out the taste, smell, gooeyness, and temperature. At the back of the brain, the occipital lobes are central in dealing with what you see. Last, but not least, your temporal lobes are active in language, hearing, memory and emotion. When you listen to music, your temporal lobes are hopping.

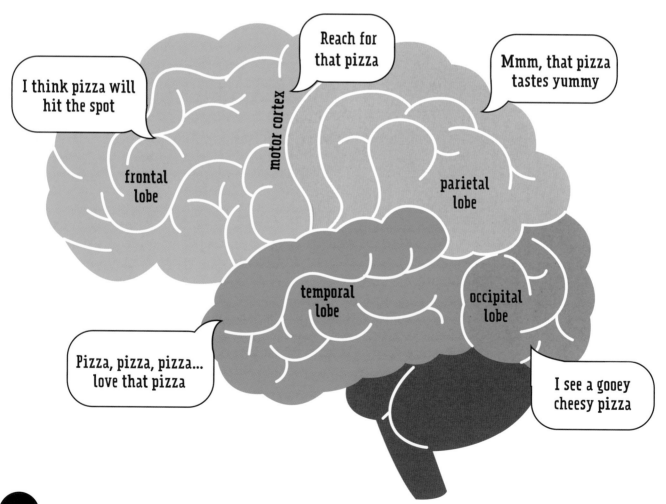

Mind and Body Working Together

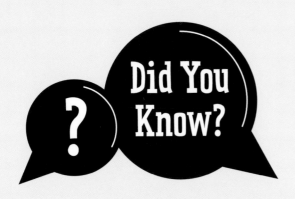
Musicophilia is an intense desire for music that is associated with brain changes or brain injury. People with musicophilia have an interest in music that is so strong it interferes with daily life because they are thinking about music all the time.

The **limbic system**, a set of brain parts tucked under the temporal lobes, is concerned with emotion. The **amygdala** is a major player in the limbic system. It is especially involved in anger, fear, and social interaction. Although it is rare, researchers were able to identify a person with a damaged amygdala. That person was not uncomfortable coming very close to another person, with noses nearly touching, invading their **personal space** in a big way. One job for the amygdala is to send out threat messages when someone stands too close.

Try This

Check out how much personal space people feel comfortable with. Using tape or chalk, mark a spot on the ground.
Stand on that spot and ask different people to come and tell you the first thing they did today. Mark where they stop to answer your question and see how the results do or don't change from person to person.

NEURONS AND HORMONES: A PARTNERSHIP

While neurons send signals to each other with the help of brain chemicals, the brain also relies on hormones to send messages. Hormones are chemical messengers that travel through the bloodstream from gland to gland. One of the most important glands is the **pituitary gland**. The pituitary gland is about the size of a pea, but it does a big job. Typically, the **hypothalamus**, a part of the limbic system of the brain, tells the pituitary gland to release hormones and together they help regulate growth, sleep, body temperature, and other important functions. Too much or too little of some hormones can affect mood.

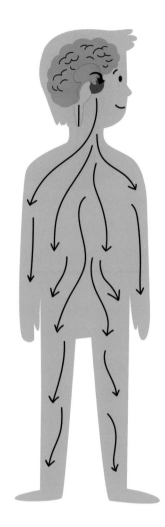

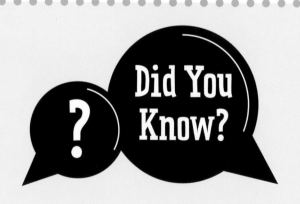

Did You Know?

When people cuddle, the hormone **oxytocin** is released. Oxytocin helps people feel good about each other, helps wounds heal, and puts you in a good mood! No wonder we sometimes feel we need a hug.

BRAIN HEALTH AND SAFETY

You probably agree that it's important to keep your brain healthy. We know that sleep, healthy foods, and exercise are good for your body, and psychologists have also shown that exercise improves certain parts of the brain and helps the neurons make good connections. Exercise will help most kids think better and do better in school because the brain itself is strengthened.

It's important that the exercise you get is safe. Many team sports can put your brain in danger, particularly those where players often run into one another, such as football or ice hockey. In other sports where players don't wear helmets, such as soccer and basketball, head injuries also occur. Even outside of team sports, kids can hurt their head falling off a bike or skateboarding. When you hit your head hard enough, you may develop a **concussion**.

A concussion is a brain injury that occurs when there is a blow to the head, enough to cause the brain to move back and forth, bounce, or twist. You may or may not black out. Symptoms include dizziness, headache, and/or feeling groggy. Even people with a mild concussion will need to sit out and rest. Concussions can cause real damage, especially if you have more than one, but nobody knows exactly how many is too many. Some rest after concussion is necessary but too much can interfere with recovery.

Check Out the Research

Pediatrician Danny Thomas, along with a team of psychologists and other specialists, studied children, adolescents, and young adults who received a head injury, came to the hospital, and were diagnosed with a concussion. The researchers asked about physical symptoms (such as headache and dizziness) and tested balance and thinking skills. The participants were randomly assigned to one of two groups: strict rest (five days of no school, work, or physical activity) and usual care (typically only one or two days of rest). Both groups returned for follow up. The researchers were surprised to find that the usual care group did better than the strict rest group. The study concluded that for mild head injury, some rest is enough with a gradual return to physical activity. A brisk walk apparently actually helps recovery, as long as the person feels up to it.

Your brain is an awesome and fascinating structure. It produces every action, memory, thought, feeling, and behavior using a complex system of connections within the brain and between the brain and the rest of the body. And the pattern of these connections is constantly changing as you learn and experience the world.

NOW YOU KNOW!

- Neuroplasticity allows the brain to benefit from experience.

- There are a variety of methods to measure the structure and activity in a live brain.

- The left side of the brain controls the right side of the body and the right side of the brain controls the left side of the body.

- The parts of the brain each play a role in different actions and behaviors.

- The brain signals which hormones are needed to keep the body working properly.

- Exercise directly improves how well the brain works.

- Some, but not too much, rest helps the brain heal after injury.

Part 3

THE ONE AND ONLY ME

Chapter 5

WHAT MAKES ME "ME"?

Who are you? Are you the kind of person who enjoys spending time on your own, or do you love being surrounded by friends? Are you a leader who likes to share your ideas, or do you hang back and scope out what others are saying? Of course, however you would answer those questions, it probably doesn't describe you all of the time. But psychologists have studied the ways different people typically act and whether, knowing this, they can predict their thoughts, feelings, and behaviors. These individual tendencies are called **personality traits.**

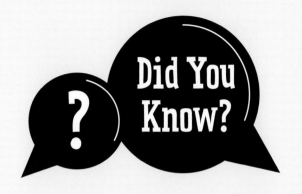

Did You Know?

There are lots of popular, unscientific ways of grouping people by personality. Have you and your friends ever talked about what animal you are like? Are you an eager beaver, playful but a good worker? A clever, curious fox? A wise owl? A loyal and friendly dog? Of course, this is all in fun but it demonstrates a way of classifying people by parts of their personality.

FIRST STEPS AT PREDICTING PERSONALITY

People have long worked to define personality types. While it sounds pretty silly to us now, in the Victorian age, physicians tried to predict personality based on the bumps on a person's head. Sigmund Freud's theory of personality, which he developed in the early part of the twentieth century, grew out of his interest in patients with symptoms he couldn't explain. He developed a complex theory that people had hidden sexual and aggressive urges they didn't even know about, but which formed their personalities. While his work didn't have scientific support, his writings launched the field of psychoanalysis, which is still practiced today. Many psychologists still value Freud's focus on the importance of early childhood experiences.

In the 1940s, psychologist William Sheldon proposed another method for predicting behavior based on body type. He suggested there were three types: ectomorphs (skinny people who were introverted, emotionally sensitive, and intellectual), endomorphs (heavier folks who were social, fun loving, and easy going), and mesomorphs (muscular people who were emotionally balanced, courageous, and strong). As you know, since psychology is a science, just coming up with a theory is only the first step. Next comes careful research to see if the theory's predictions are accurate. Scientific studies of Sheldon's theory did not support his hypothesis, and it is no longer taken seriously by psychologists.

MORE USEFUL WAYS TO DESCRIBE PERSONALITY

In the first half of the twentieth century, Gordon Allport and Henry S. Odbert took a different approach. They thought that an individual's personality resulted from a combination of different traits. As a starting point, they developed a list of over 17,000 words that could be used to describe a person's character. Later researchers worked to determine how these descriptions might be grouped in ways that were simpler but still useful in describing people and predicting behavior.

One of the most famous of these psychologists was Raymond Cattell. He gathered data about a large group of people based on their school and work records, their answers to questions about themselves, and tests designed to look at their beliefs and values. After a lot of research, Dr. Cattell used data analysis methods to see what behaviors seemed to happen together in the same people. Based on his findings he proposed 16 main personality traits that were different from one another and useful in predicting behavior. He developed a test called the 16PF (16 Personality Factors Test) that could be used to help determine a person's personality traits.

Did You Know?

If you look at social media or read magazines, you've probably run into quizzes that claim to describe your personality. How do they get away with such an unscientific test? The **Barnum effect** provides a clue. A few different psychologists have studied people's tendency to believe general statements about themselves, such as "you have a great need for other people to admire you" and "you have a tendency to be critical of yourself"—things that are true of most people! Advertisers use the Barnum effect to draw you in. Barnum refers to P.T. Barnum, the founder of the Barnum & Bailey Circus, a master of verbal trickery.

Research by later psychologists suggested that Cattell's 16 personality categories were still too many. In fact, most psychologists now focus on "the big five" basic personality traits. A person can be at one end or the other of each of these traits, or they can be somewhere in the middle.

In order to confirm that personality measurements are useful, psychologists have to be sure that repeated testings give the same results—that is, that they show **reliability**. And they need to show that the tests measure what they are designed to measure, which is known as **construct validity**. Psychologists have done lots of research confirming that where people fall on the big five personality traits is stable over time and useful in predicting a variety of different behaviors across many cultures.

Big Five
Personality Traits

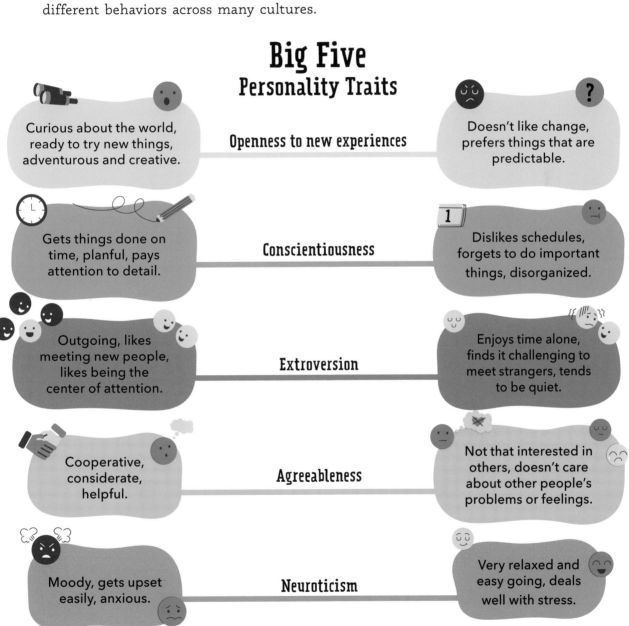

Curious about the world, ready to try new things, adventurous and creative.	**Openness to new experiences** · Doesn't like change, prefers things that are predictable.
Gets things done on time, planful, pays attention to detail.	**Conscientiousness** · Dislikes schedules, forgets to do important things, disorganized.
Outgoing, likes meeting new people, likes being the center of attention.	**Extroversion** · Enjoys time alone, finds it challenging to meet strangers, tends to be quiet.
Cooperative, considerate, helpful.	**Agreeableness** · Not that interested in others, doesn't care about other people's problems or feelings.
Moody, gets upset easily, anxious.	**Neuroticism** · Very relaxed and easy going, deals well with stress.

As a trick to remember the "big five," notice that the first letters of each word combine to spell "OCEAN".

While personality traits influence how a person acts, it doesn't mean that those behaviors happen all the time. Research psychologist William Fleeson was interested in what would happen if someone pretended to have different personality traits. He knew that extroverted people tend to be happier overall than people who are introverted (the opposite of extroverted). He had some extroverted and some introverted participants act extroverted during a ten-minute conversation. Not only could all of his participants act extroverted, but they all reported feeling happier after doing so—even the introverts!

Try This

Most real people don't fall at the extremes of the big five personality traits, but may tend toward one end or the other. On the other hand, fictional characters are often portrayed more simply. Take a favorite character from a book, movie, or TV show that you like. How would you describe them based upon the "big five"? Here's an example to get you started:

Big Bird — This easy-going guy is very *agreeable*. He's kind and works well with others and is as helpful as he can be. He's also very *open to new experiences* and eager to learn from those around him. He's pretty *extroverted* and likes to meet new people but he doesn't try to grab a lot of attention, so he's probably in the middle on this trait.

Oscar the Grouch — Definitely *not an agreeable* sort. Oscar is grumpy and seems mostly interested in himself, not other people. Oscar is also *not very extroverted*. It seems sometimes he'd be happiest if everyone left him alone.

Notice how there are times, however, when these characters step out of character. While their personality traits are extreme, sometimes circumstances have a big impact on their behavior. There are times when even Oscar the Grouch can be kind and thoughtful!

PERSONALITY TRAITS AREN'T THE WHOLE STORY

Maybe you can think of a classmate who is quiet in new situations (towards the lower end of "extroversion"), very responsible and good at following through on assignments (pretty high on "conscientiousness"), and pretty easy going (high on "agreeableness"). It would make sense to choose that person as a partner for a very important school project. But, if that classmate was sick, distracted by a big family problem, or had some other big problem in their life, that situation might have more of an influence on their behavior than their personality. Psychologist Walter Mischel studied the research on personality traits and found that, while traits were useful in predicting behavior, they weren't enough by themselves. Changes to a person's circumstances also mattered a *lot*.

People are pretty aware of that when thinking about themselves, but less so when trying to understand other people. Richard Nisbett and his research team found that people are more confident when describing the traits of other people than when using them to label themselves. They are far more likely to say, "it depends on the situation" when asked which of two labels more accurately described themselves than when asked to describe someone else.

Did You Know?

"Being smart, you don't believe that a cookie can teach you about yourself"

People may think personality traits can't be changed, but behavior is often better predicted by a person's situation. This may be why people believe the fortunes in fortune cookies, horoscopes, or palm-reading. These messages stick to (usually positive) descriptions of ways that most people would react to a situation, fooling us into thinking they accurately described our personalities.

ARE YOU JUST BORN THAT WAY?

Has anyone in your family said that you are a lot like a parent or other family member? Are those similarities due to inheritance? Maybe you and your mom or dad are similar because you share the same genes. But family members often also share similar lifestyles, experiences, and relationships with other relatives. So, is personality inborn and biological, or is it something that develops from experiences? As you learned in Chapter 2, research using twins is helpful in answering this huge question.

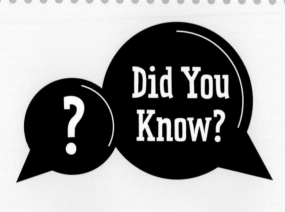

The question of *"nature versus nurture"* is an important focus of a lot of research in psychology (as well as medicine, biology, and other areas of science). Research showing the importance of genes and biological processes highlights the importance of nature. Although the word "nurture" is used in everyday language to mean adults taking care of young children, in this case "nurture" is used to refer to any early influences, including things like parents' methods for teaching kids, how many books and educational experiences a child has, bad life experiences, and even exposure to nutritious foods or poisons and pollution.

Studies of twins demonstrate the importance of biology in determining personality. Fraternal twins of the same gender share many experiences, but are no more alike genetically than siblings who are not twins. Identical twins, however, share both similar experiences and exactly the same genes. Studies of twin babies have shown that identical twins share many more tendencies that could be early signs of personality types, including their tendencies to cry or be fidgety, than do fraternal twins.

Psychologist Nancy Segal, a twin herself, has spent years studying twins. She talks about one set of identical twins raised apart since they were babies. Both became volunteer firemen. Both had jobs where they installed systems in buildings (one to put out fires, the other burglar alarms). Both wore big belts with big buckles and keys hanging off of them, and both always carried a knife.

While stories like this tempt us to think that a lot of behavior must be genetic, Dr. Segal also reminds us that the twins' behavior also changes how they are treated by others and those interactions become part of their experience. So, a baby who is very active and likes excitement (which may indeed be genetic) is likely to push parents to find active things for them to do. Being exposed to more active experiences may then lead the twins to adult interests that require bravery in the face of danger—like fighting fires.

In addition to studies on identical twins, research on the consistency of traits over adulthood and research looking at how tiny infants' reactions to stress predicts later traits support the importance of genes in determining personality. Very exciting research connecting specific genes to levels of certain brain chemicals, which are linked to patterns of behavior, suggest that someday scientists may be able to know a lot more about inborn aspects of personality.

THE IMPORTANCE OF "NURTURE"

While psychologists generally agree that genes have an important impact on personality, that's not the whole story. Even identical twins don't have exactly the same personalities. In fact, research suggests that they appear very similar on personality tests less than half of the time (but still much more similar than non-identical siblings). So, what else leads to development of personality traits?

Many psychologists of the past had theories about how early experiences shaped the development of a child's personality. In Chapter 7 of this book you'll meet behaviorists John Watson and B.F. Skinner, who studied how behaviors could be learned through pairing two events or by rewarding certain behaviors. Both felt that early learning experiences could set a child up to react in certain ways to later experiences.

Albert Bandura's focus on children learning by watching others and copying those behaviors is another way personality is formed. Bandura also noted that once personality starts to develop, a child's consistent behaviors impact those around them and can lead others to behave in ways that support that learning. For example, if a baby tends to smile and babble a lot when people talk to them, adults around them will find that fun. They are then likely to put more energy into talking to and making faces at the baby, which the baby will find rewarding. He called this **reciprocal determinism**. In this circular pattern personality traits, as well as the behaviors of others that encourage them, are continually reinforced and likely to happen again.

Check Out the Research

The impact of experiences may depend on the personality traits of the people experiencing them. Patrick Markey's research looked at measures of hostility in teenagers after watching violent video games. Their responses depended upon their personalities. Teens who were high in neuroticism, less agreeable, and less conscientious seemed to have the greatest increase in hostility after playing the games. Kids who were emotionally stable, agreeable, and conscientious were only mildly impacted.

Although a person's personality tends to stay consistent, this doesn't mean there are no changes as a person goes through life. In fact, there are predictable ways in which adults change over time (becoming more conscientious and agreeable and less neurotic). A big time for changes in personality is in young adulthood. And research shows that people can make helpful changes to their personality through therapy and consistent practice.

Thinking about what another person is like can help us to understand them and know what to expect of them. Research has helped narrow down categories of personality traits that are consistent and predict different kinds of behavior. While personality appears to be based in part on our biology, it is also heavily influenced by experience. Personality traits are helpful in describing a person's behavior over time, but people are also impacted by what is happening around them and that is likely to be a strong predictor of their behavior in a specific situation.

The One and Only Me

NOW YOU KNOW!

○ Psychologists' early attempts to develop useful methods to predict personality sometimes focused on physical differences between people. Research found that this approach was not very useful.

○ Many research studies led to groupings of descriptions of personality that were consistent and predicted behavior. These groupings are called personality traits.

○ These days most psychologists agree on five personality traits, "the big five."

○ Research findings done on biologically-related people suggest that genes play an important role in personality. Studies with identical twins have been especially useful in this research.

○ While genes are important, they do not control personality on their own. Life experiences, especially early ones, also contribute to personality traits.

○ Personality traits are not permanently set. Some change in predictable ways as a person gets older and others can be changed through active effort.

Chapter 6

WHAT DOES IT MEAN TO BE A BOY OR A GIRL?

One of the first questions people ask when a baby is born (or even before) is "Is it a boy or a girl?" When asking this, people appear to be interested in basic biology: whether the baby has a penis or a vagina. Based on this information, they will conclude what **sex** the baby is: "male" or "female." You can see what a baby looks like when they are born, but sex also includes genes, hormones, and other biological influences.

But people are interested in more than biology. They are curious about what the baby's **gender** will be. A person's gender refers to society's expectations of how a person will think, feel, and act. Words like "boy," "girl," "man," and "woman" are common words to describe someone's gender. (There are other words too, and we'll talk about them later on in this chapter.) Gender is a personal identity that's a lot more complex than simple biology.

There are lots of gender **stereotypes** based on how people think "girls" or "boys" should look or act. Being a boy or girl can influence what others think of you and even what you think of yourself. For example, boys may feel they should always be strong and avoid expressing their needs or fears. Girls may feel they should be the ones to take care of others and not get angry or argue.

Try This

When someone first meets you, how do you think they would describe you? Is part of that description whether you are a girl or a boy? What else might they notice about you based upon how you look?

Based on how you appear, might people make assumptions about:

- What shows, games, and music you do or don't like?

- What clothes you like to wear?

- Whether you prefer to be outdoors or indoors?

- What you can or can't do well?

Do you think some of these assumptions are due to your gender? Would any of them be wrong? Would any of them give an incomplete impression of you? It is natural to put people into categories (like boy or girl), but in doing so, it is likely that others will make assumptions that aren't true of you.

BOY OR GIRL?

Most children identify themselves as a boy or a girl by age 2 ½. Even young kids see gender as an important part of who they are. As preschoolers, children develop an awareness of gender stereotypes that have a strong influence on their behavior by the time they start elementary school. While toddlers happily play with a variety of toys, preferences change as they get a bit older. Boys will tend toward boy-stereotyped toys and clothes and avoid "girl things" and, although girls tend to be interested in a wider variety of play objects, they are more likely to participate in girl-stereotyped activities than boys are and to prefer "girl" clothes. Very young children, who are working hard to learn important categories for defining themselves and others, can be extra strict about their ideas of gender.

"This is the Daddy block, this is the Mommy block, this is the baby block"

Try This

Ask your parent, grandparent, or other adult who knew you when you were very little if you were ever insistent that something that was just for a boy or just for a girl. Does it surprise you to learn that you once felt that way?

The One and Only Me

In the next chapter you will read about social learning. Psychologists, like social learning theorist Albert Bandura, suggest that these differences in boy/girl behavior result from watching what other people of the same gender do and how those in a child's environment treat them differently based upon their gender. In fact, a number of studies in the 1970's and 1980's showed that children often got negative reactions from parents and even other kids if they chose to play with toys seen as not appropriate for their gender. Knowledge of these research findings was widely discussed in the news and led some parents to actively encourage children to play with toys not traditionally seen as gender appropriate. Kids, however, often continued to choose play that fit gender stereotypes.

Toys for boys or girls?

Check Out the Research

Researcher Kristin Shutts and colleagues showed three-year-old children videos of other kids giving their opinions about new kinds of clothing, toys, and food. When the children were then asked which of the items they liked, they tended to prefer the same ones as kids in the video who were the same gender.

STEREOTYPES AND UNWRITTEN RULES

While it appears that there are some differences in abilities between the sexes, they are often less extreme than many people believe. Some may be due as much to gender stereotypes and expectations as to biology. Stereotypes and prejudice impact such important aspects of life as education, ability to work at certain jobs, the amount of money a person earns, and who gets custody of children after a divorce. Some people even think a person's sex or gender should determine the sex or gender of the people they are romantically or sexually attracted to. But really, gender and sexual orientation are two completely separate topics.

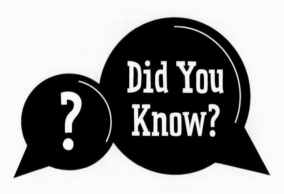

Although the roles of men and women in families were rigid in the past, they have also been changeable. During colonial times, fathers had authority over the family with absolute rights of custody to their children. Books about how to raise children were written for fathers, not mothers. By the 1900s beliefs about men, women, and children had changed so dramatically that mothers were seen as the primary parent. Child-rearing books then were written for mothers and, in the case of divorce, mothers more often got custody of children. Nowadays it's accepted that both fathers and mothers are important to children. When parents divorce, they usually share custody of their children.

In the United States it is believed that both boys and girls should go to school, but this isn't true throughout the world. In some places, girls cannot get an education due to gender stereotypes. Their families may have to pay for school and feel that it's a waste of money to educate girls since they will spend their lives taking care of a house and children. Or, girls may already have many chores at home and not have time for school. What do you think it would be like for someone your age not to be able to read, write, or do math because of the expectations for people of their gender?

The One and Only Me

Read in the library or online for information about Malala Yousafzai, a girl from Pakistan who was brutally attacked because she spoke out for the rights of girls to be educated. Even after she was terribly hurt, she continues to fight for the rights of girls.

In the past, math and science were seen as subjects that boys were better at than girls. But that assumption is changing. As cultural expectations have changed, so have girls' math performance! In 1983, in the group of students who scored at the top in math, there were 13 boys for every girl. In 2007, while boys still outnumbered girls, the difference was closer to 3 to one.

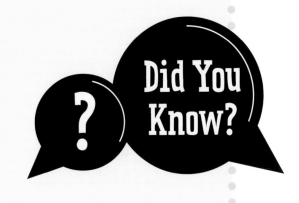

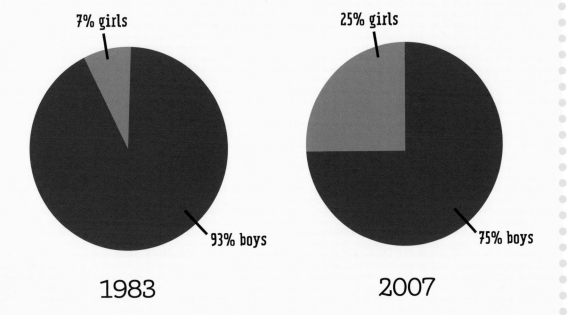

7% girls

93% boys

1983

25% girls

75% boys

2007

What Does It Mean to Be a Boy or a Girl?

Assumptions based on stereotypes have a big impact not only on education, but also on the type of job a person can get once they have an education. In the past, women were not allowed to have certain jobs, and other jobs were seen as inappropriate for men. These attitudes have changed over the years, but hidden social pressures still impact the types of jobs men and women do.

Comparison of Women and Men in Certain Jobs as of 2010

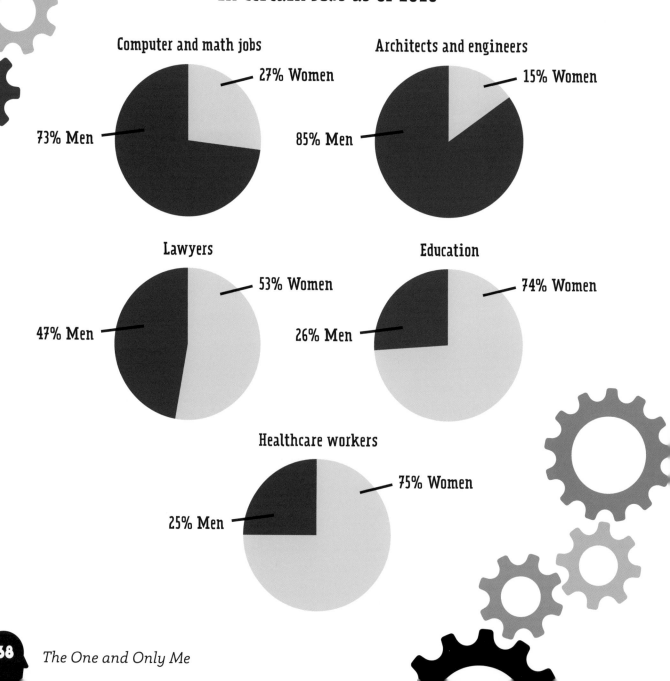

Computer and math jobs
27% Women
73% Men

Architects and engineers
15% Women
85% Men

Lawyers
53% Women
47% Men

Education
74% Women
26% Men

Healthcare workers
75% Women
25% Men

The One and Only Me

Even when women outnumber men in a workplace, they tend to make less money and have less power than the men working there. For example, while there are far more women who work in healthcare than men, there are far fewer women in the highest positions—those who run hospitals or healthcare organizations. Doctors and nurses who are women on average make less money than doctors and nurses who are men. Psychologists are studying attitudes and behaviors that cause the gender pay gap so that they can make recommendations for greater fairness.

Check Out the Research

When a group of executives in a workshop were asked to draw a picture of a leader, most of them drew a man. But is that because men are more likely to be leaders? Or is it just because others expect them to be and notice when they are? A study by psychologists Madeline Heilman and Michelle Haynes had participants in a research study read descriptions of work completed by pairs of men and women and evaluate the workers. They found that the women in the pairs were less likely to be seen as competent or as leaders even though the descriptions didn't provide details that might lead to that conclusion.

WHEN GENDER IDENTITY AND BIOLOGY DON'T FIT EXPECTATIONS

One way stereotypes have been harmful is when sex at birth doesn't match a person's **gender identity**, their sense of themself. For example, **transgender** individuals are assigned one sex at birth, but feel deeply that they are the other. Pressures to fit into what is expected of them based upon their sex (and therefore, what people think their gender *should* be) can be extremely stressful. Transgender kids and adults are often subject to teasing, bullying, and even physical attacks. Other people may try to stop them from dressing or fixing their hair in a way that fits their identity. Even using their preferred bathroom can raise resistance from other people. It is very important that parents, friends, and others accept the person as the gender they identify as.

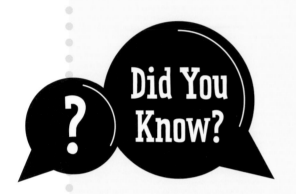

Did You Know?

In some cultures, transgender people have been accepted and seen for centuries as being a third gender between male and female. In East India, transgender people are called "hijra." The Navajo nation refers to them as "two spirited."

Who you are as a person is strongly influenced by whether you identify as a boy or a girl. For most people (but not everyone) those gender identities are consistent with their biological sex. Beliefs and expectations about gender can lead to different experiences for boys and girls and men and women. These differences occur in views on how you should or shouldn't act, what you can and can't do, and how you should look. Gender expectations can also result in different challenges and opportunities in school and the work world.

The One and Only Me

NOW YOU KNOW

- Sex is a label based on biological characteristics.

- Gender is a cultural label, based on assumptions and attitudes of how people of different sexes should look, act, think, and feel. It is also a personal identity.

- Gender stereotypes affect schools and the workplace.

- For some people, the sex they were assigned at birth does not fit with the gender they identify as. When that feeling is very strong, the person may be psychologically healthier and happier living as their gender identity.

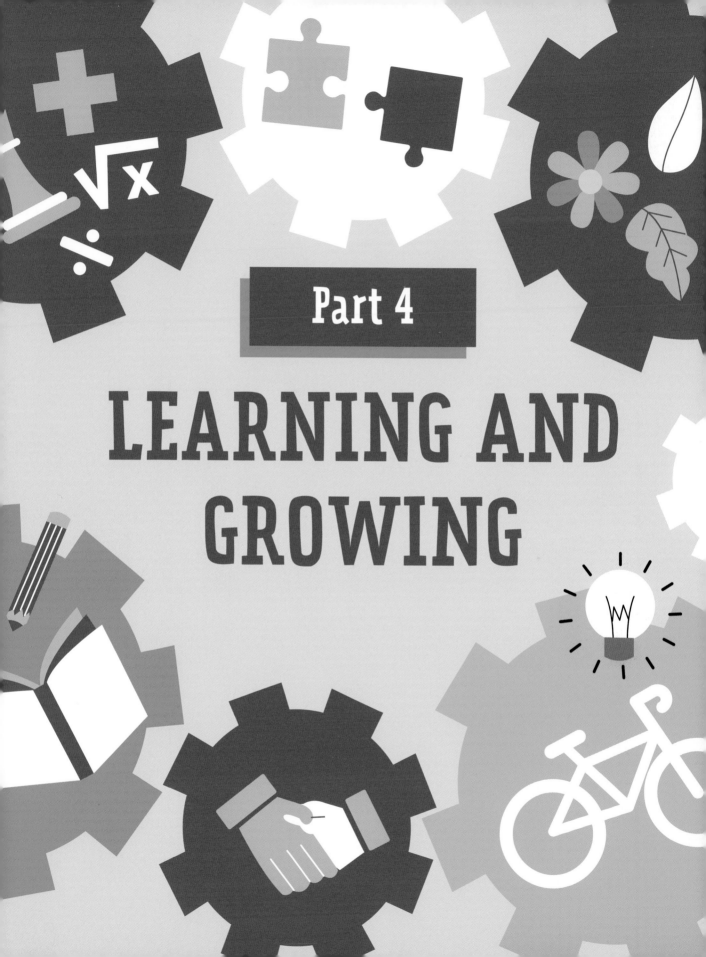

Part 4

LEARNING AND GROWING

Chapter 7

HOW DID YOU LEARN THAT?

From the day you're born, you're learning—new skills, new words, new behaviors, new information, and more. Sometimes you know you are learning. You read about something you didn't know before, a hockey coach demonstrates how to dribble, a parent teaches you how to fill the dishwasher, or you use YouTube to discover how to draw an airplane.

These are paths to learning, to new stored knowledge and abilities. But there are paths to learning that are less obvious. Early psychologists wanted to know how new learning takes place. Through their research, they described important principles of learning.

In the late 1800s, Ivan Pavlov studied learning that happens by association. He showed that a natural response (a reflex you are born with) can become paired with a new response. This kind of paired learning is called **classical conditioning**. Pavlov received a Nobel Prize for his work in 1904.

Check Out the Research

Pavlov observed that dogs drooled in response to meat. When he rang a bell, they had no reaction. But then he rang a bell over and over just before he gave his dogs meat. Soon, he could ring the bell without the meat, and the dogs would drool. The dogs learned that the bell was a signal that meat was coming.

LEARNING GONE WRONG

Like Pavlov's dogs, you might be conditioned to get hungry when the lunch bell rings at school. Beware: some classical conditioning is unpleasant. For example, say you ate green Jello, and soon after you got a stomach bug that made you throw up. The pairing of the Jello and the stomach bug might make you feel like throwing up the next time you see green Jello. A behavior scientist, John Watson, showed how this unpleasant classical conditioning works in a famous 1920 experiment on a baby named "little Albert".

Check Out the Research

Dr. John Watson noticed that Albert wasn't afraid of a pet white rat, but that he jumped in fear and cried when Dr. Watson took a hammer and clanged a pipe very loudly nearby (of course he did!). In this experiment, over and over again, he showed Albert the pet rat. Then he made the clanging noise. After a while, Albert didn't need the clanging to get scared. He got upset just at the sight of the rat. And, what's more, Albert started to be afraid of lots of white furry things, including a rabbit, a dog, a fur coat, cotton balls, and a Santa mask. Poor little Albert! This experiment would not be done today because it was harmful, but it is still a famous example of classical conditioning.

As you see, not all learning is helpful! People learn to be afraid of things that are not dangerous. Maybe you got a bee sting and you worried about going outside after that. But there is good news: Fear can be unlearned. To unlearn fear, the association needs to weaken. For example, you need to see bees and not get stung. Lots of good experiences outdoors will help you unlearn your fear.

Try This

Ask someone if they'd be willing to be in an experiment. Stand behind them and use a ruler to tap a table three times and then gently tap the person on the head. Repeat this pairing many times. Then tap the table four times. Did your volunteer jump a little, expecting a tap on the head?

OR This

Ring a bell and then feed your pet. Repeat this ring/feed sequence several times and see if your pet comes when you ring the bell. (If your pet is a fish, you can still do this experiment. Instead of a bell, put your finger on one spot on the tank and wait until your fish is near it to feed them.)

HOW IS A LOLLIPOP LIKE A DOG BISCUIT?

Classical conditioning is limited because it relies on a natural response to a natural action. Building on Pavlov's work, researchers studied a different kind of learning. This type of learning happens as a consequence of your behavior. To understand how it works, consider this riddle: *How is a lollipop like a dog biscuit?*

The answer is that each can make it more likely that a behavior will happen again; of course, dog biscuits work best for dogs, and lollipops for kids. Have you ever seen a dog trainer give a pet a treat after they followed a command? That trainer is using the same kind of learning science that parents use when they reward their kid with a treat, like a lollipop, for helping them with grocery shopping.

Some kinds of rewards are automatically pleasing to most everyone: delicious food, water if you're thirsty, cuddling or hugs, and so forth. Other kinds of items or experiences become rewarding because you've come to associate them (through conditioning) with these basic rewards, or because you've come to learn that they can be used to get what you want. So, with experience, praise, coins for a snack machine, stickers on a chart, and other items can become rewarding.

The learning process that uses rewards is known as **operant conditioning**.

Check Out the Research

One of the first psychologists to study operant conditioning was B.F. Skinner. He was interested in showing that learning is a step-by-step process of behavior followed by reward. In the 1930's, he built experimental cages that he called "Skinner boxes" and studied operant conditioning using rats and birds. In some of his experiments, he found that rats could learn to push a bar if they got a little piece of food each time. The first time the rat hit the bar was an accident, but, after getting a reward, the rats quickly learned that pushing the bar meant getting food. They would go over to the bar as soon as they were put in the box.

Skinner also explored teaching animals more difficult kinds of behaviors that they'd never done before. He and his colleagues found that they could teach animals to do many new and surprising things by rewarding small steps along the way. This gradual building of more complicated behaviors is called **shaping**. For example, to teach pigeons to play ping pong, they started by giving the birds a bit of food each time their beaks touched a ping pong ball. Once they learned that behavior, the next step was to give them a treat for pushing the ball upward. Little by little, the birds learned to hit a ping pong ball back and forth to one another!

Look up B.F. Skinner to find out what unusual work he did with pigeons during World War II.

Explore Further

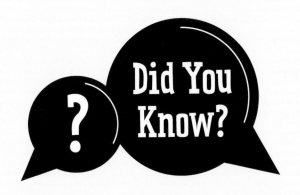

? Did You Know?

While teaching pigeons to play ping pong is kind of silly, these experiments showed that animals could learn pretty complicated skills. Today service dogs play an important role in the lives of many people. By rewarding small steps, service animals can learn to help blind people move around obstacles, open and close doors, alert hearing-impaired owners to sounds, help pull a wheelchair, and more. Military and police dogs can be trained to sniff for illegal drugs and hidden bombs.

Try This

Volunteer to participate in your own experiment. Ask an adult if they are willing to set up rewards for you to make it more likely that you follow through on a behavior (like practicing a sport, musical instrument, or artistic talent; eating more healthy food; or keeping schoolwork organized). Talk to them about rewards (like a later bedtime once a week, a treat, or family game time). Set goals, which can be daily or weekly. Ask your adult to help you track your progress and reward you when you meet your goals. You may find that your goal gets easier and easier when you get rewards.

A TREAT BEATS A SCOLDING

Of course, if something unpleasant follows a behavior, the behavior is *less* likely to be repeated, at least for a little while. This is the idea behind punishment. It works to reduce a behavior, but it turns out that punishment is not as effective or long lasting at helping you reach a goal as positive rewards.

If you ever helped to train a pet, you used these learning methods. Both rewards and punishments are often used in animal training. But remember, psychologists have found that punishments only work for a little while, while rewards tend to lead to more lasting changes. So, if you are training your pet or if you are trying to help yourself develop a new good habit, you might want to think about what behaviors you want to teach rather than which ones you want to stop. Using rewards more than punishments requires some creative thinking. In the case of training a dog, for example, it's important to reward the dog when they signal that they need to go out to pee, and not just punish them when they have an accident.

Your teacher probably uses rewards and punishments in your classroom. Many teachers use praise or other rewards to encourage kids to raise their hands and answer questions in class. Or, a teacher may give the class a pizza party for reading a certain number of books or being quiet during an assembly. What rewards do you notice in your classroom?

BABY SEE, BABY DO

Rachel was visiting her three-year-old cousin, Zach. She thought it was so cute to watch him pretend to cook. How did he learn to stir the pot and pour the tea? Not all learning happens through classical or operant conditioning. Learning can also happen through watching others perform actions. This kind of learning is called **modeling**.

Check Out the Research

In a famous modeling experiment, psychologist **Albert Bandura** set up a bobo doll, a large plastic figure filled with air with a weight on the bottom. If you knock it over, it pops back up. The researchers had some children watch an adult hit the doll angrily, and some children watch an adult behave gently. Then they put the children one at a time in a room with a bobo doll. The children who saw the angry adult hit the doll hard also hit the doll hard, and the children who had seen the adult act gently were gentle themselves.

Of course, not everyone who watches violence acts violently, but now you know why your parents and teachers worry about games and videos that include violence.

Try This

Try greeting your teacher each day in a foreign language. You can say "Bonjour" or "Buenos días." Don't explain it to anyone, just smile and keep it up. Does anyone begin to use your greeting? If they do, they learned by watching!

WHAT DOES IT MEAN?

Although learning experiments with animals can explain some behaviors in humans, it seems that early psychologists who developed their ideas working with animals missed something. For example, in one experiment, monkeys who saw other monkeys receive a better reward quit responding. Rewards don't always work as expected. For people, the meaning of rewards and thoughts about behavior can be important. Later scientific studies found that sometimes kids who got a reward, like a trophy or money, actually became less interested in the activity! It's best when the activity itself is rewarding. If you feel good about the activity you are doing, you are more likely to do the activity more often.

NOW YOU KNOW!

○ Ivan Pavlov used classical conditioning to teach dogs to drool when they heard a bell. His work influenced many scientists to explore the process of learning.

○ John Watson demonstrated that classical conditioning could lead little Albert to be afraid of white fluffy things.

○ Fears that are learned can be unlearned.

○ With operant conditioning, you are more likely to engage in a behavior if something pleasant (a reward) follows it. When punishment follows a behavior, the behavior is less likely to happen again, but the result may be temporary. Using rewards to change behavior lasts longer than using punishment.

○ Shaping is training a new, complicated behavior by rewarding small steps along the way.

○ Albert Bandura used modeling to show how people can learn behaviors by watching others.

Chapter 8

WHAT DOES IT MEAN TO BE SMART?

People have a lot of different ideas of what it means to be smart. To some, being smart means getting all the answers right on tests or getting high grades. But what about putting together amazing building block structures? Or playing a musical instrument, or speaking a second language? Psychologists study what it means to be intelligent.

Most agree that human **intelligence** is:

- How well someone learns from their experiences.

- Whether a person can think about and control the way they think so that they use their abilities well.

- How flexible someone is in their thinking. Can they try a different approach if a situation changes?

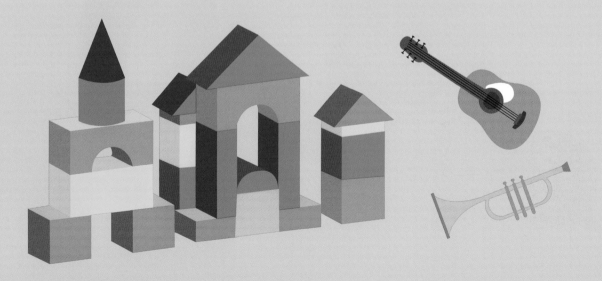

Researchers refer to some parts of intelligence as **crystallized intelligence** (knowledge you've learned and can pull out and use when you need it) and some as **fluid intelligence** (thinking logically, identifying patterns, and solving unfamiliar problems).

What people consider intelligent varies across cultures, which have different environments and experiences. For example, Dr. Robert Serpell, a psychologist in Zambia, Africa, gave tasks to children who were similar in most ways (all from cities, same sorts of family circumstances) but one group was from England and one group was from Zambia. He gave the kids figures to copy. The English kids did better on a paper-and-pencil form. The Zambian kids did better with wire modeling (Zambian kids often use wire to make things). Is one group more intelligent than the other? No, they have different experiences that have shaped their abilities. But what if a kid from Zambia went to England, or a kid from England went to Zambia? Would they seem less intelligent just because they are in a different place? As you read and think about what it means to be smart, keep in mind that it is impossible to have a definition of intelligence that is free from one's growing-up experiences.

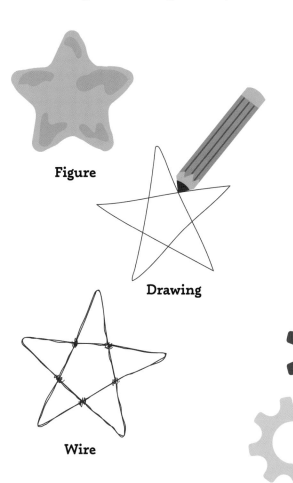

Figure

Drawing

Wire

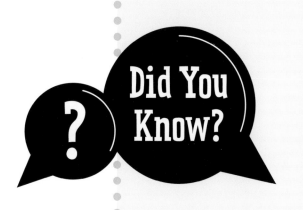

Did You Know?

Psychologists who first explored ways of measuring intelligence came up with a score they called an Intelligence Quotient, or IQ. Early developers of IQ tests for children tried to determine if a child's abilities on those tests were at a level expected for kids of their age. If so, they would have an IQ of 100, which is average. Today's tests are still constructed with a 100 IQ as the middle of the average range.

CAN WE TEST INTELLIGENCE?

In order to be able to research a psychological concept, you need not only a definition, but also a way to measure it. The field of intelligence testing traces its roots to the work of French psychologists Alfred Binet and Theodore Simon, who created a test in the early 1900s to separate average learners from learners who needed extra help in school. Their work was taken further in the United States by Lewis Terman, of Stanford University. For years, the Stanford-Binet test, first published in 1916, was the standard for intelligence tests. The original test has been updated through the decades and it is still used today. This intelligence test, and others like it, includes puzzles, how items are similar or different, what words mean, number memory, and so forth.

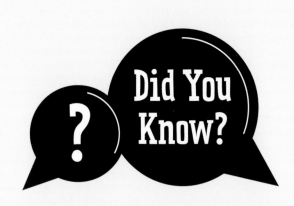

Did You Know?

Many employers ask job applicants to take an IQ test—even the National Football League (NFL). Draft picks not only have to show that they are stand-out players, but they have to answer questions designed to test their intelligence.

There is controversy about what test scores actually mean and whether they are helpful or hurtful. Kids from disadvantaged neighborhoods with lower quality schools are not getting the same experiences as kids with more advantages. Maybe test scores reflect those unfair differences and not actual intelligence.

Remember that when Binet and Simon were developing their test, they had a practical reason for doing so: identifying children who needed help in school. IQ scores do predict grades and school achievement: in general, the higher the IQ, the higher the grades and the further in school one gets. But scores can be misleading.

What doesn't an IQ score predict? IQ is not meant to predict a person's goodness or how much a person will contribute to making the world a better place. It doesn't tell anything about making good decisions or having common sense. Intelligence testing provides one kind of information, but nowhere near all the information about the skills needed to succeed in life.

Lots of kids think having a high IQ means someone will do well at anything, but you also need other skills (like being a hard worker or working well with other people) to be successful. And, interestingly, some kids with an extremely high IQ struggle to fit in because they aren't interested in the same things as other kids. People tend to think that a high IQ is more important than it really is! Also, IQ tests can include information or tasks that kids from some backgrounds aren't familiar with because they've never been exposed to them before. Some kids of color or kids from less affluent communities might be smarter than IQ tests can show. IQ tests are not always a good measure of intelligence. There are theories of multiple intelligence that go beyond an IQ score.

Check Out the Research

Psychologists wondered whether being told a kid was especially smart would change how adults acted towards them and make a difference in how well the kids actually did. In 1963, Robert Rosenthal and Lenore Jackson tested elementary school children on an IQ test. They then selected a portion of the children at random and told their teachers that they were gifted students who were expected to do especially well in school. At the end of the school year, they re-tested the children. Those children who had been labeled as high IQ regardless of their actual scores in fact showed significantly greater gains in IQ than the children in the control group. When teachers expected particular children to do well, they did!

In addition to teachers' expectations, a person's surroundings, motivation, and life experiences can have an impact on IQ test scores. Think about different sizes of rubber bands. They represent the intelligence you were born with. With positive family experiences, access to books and learning, good schools, etc., the rubber band can stretch pretty far!

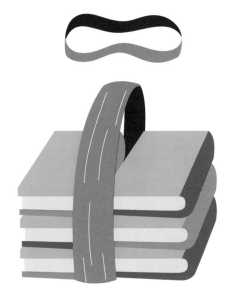

MORE THAN ONE WAY TO BE SMART

In order to make the concept of intelligence more useful than a single IQ score, many psychologists developed theories of what intelligence is. Psychologists are not in agreement about these theories, but each has received a lot of attention.

Some, like Howard Gardner, proposed that intelligence is a group of abilities, known as **multiple intelligences**.

Howard Gardner's Theory of Eight Intelligences

KIND OF INTELLIGENCE	DESCRIPTION	EXAMPLES
Word smart	thinking and solving problems with words	writing, word games, speeches
Logic smart	reasoning with logic, patterns, and numbers	chess, computers, math
Picture smart	dealing with information in pictures and 3-D space	puzzles, structures, maps
Music smart	thinking through sound and musical patterns	playing and writing music
Body smart	relating to the world through touch and movement	athletics, dance, gymnastics
People smart	relating to and understanding other people	group activities, leadership
Self smart	awareness of feelings, ideas, goals	creating journals, setting personal goals
Nature smart	natural interest in and knowledge about the environment	classifying rocks, identifying plants

People might have more than one of these areas of strength. While Gardner's model needs more research support, it influenced many people to broaden their view of what it means to be intelligent.

Try This

Think about your strengths and weaknesses. Using Gardner's model, what do you consider your top three intelligences? Draw a diagram like the one below on a separate sheet of paper.

My Smarts

....	....	....
....	....	....

Have a parent or teacher select the three they think best describe you. Did they choose the same three you chose? Did the concept of multiple intelligences change how you think about what makes someone smart?

Another way of thinking about intelligence is Robert Sternberg's **triarchic theory of human intelligence** that focuses on how effectively a person deals with the world around them. He was interested in an individual's analytical, practical, and creative abilities. Analytical looks at how you solve problems. Practical is how well you apply and use knowledge. Creative is about thinking in new ways.

ANALYTICAL	Describe how two pieces of music are the same and different.
PRACTICAL	Choose a song to help a group of kindergarten students calm down.
CREATIVE	Write a song.

Research shows that funny people are more intelligent. Not only do funny people make others laugh, they laugh more themselves, which releases helpful brain chemicals that are healthy for the body. Research shows that watching a funny video improved performance on problem-solving tasks. Humor can be a kind of brain exercise! But that doesn't mean you should watch cat videos instead of doing your homework...

ALL ABOUT THINKING

The field of study that examines how people think and learn is known as **cognitive psychology**. Cognitive psychologists study how we are capable of thinking, remembering, perceiving, and learning through words and images. As we take in and deal with information in various ways, our brains organize the information and help us make sense of the world around us.

Language is an important way that we communicate our knowledge and thoughts to others by talking (or signing), reading, or writing. Language is also part of what sets humans apart from other animals. We know that animals have some ability to communicate, but a complete language system, an organized means of combining words to communicate, is only seen in humans. Language has basic characteristics and purposes that are similar across the globe, although languages also have interesting differences. For example, Peter Gordon did experiments with members of the Piraha tribe in Brazil. He found that they have only three number words: for one, two, and many. He found that they had trouble on counting and matching tasks on quantities larger than three, suggesting that math thinking is affected by the lack of a counting system in the language.

Explore Further

Look up videos of Kanzi, a bonobo, who psychologist Sue Savage-Rumbaugh taught to communicate. How is Kanzi's language like a human's and how is it different? Do you think Kanzi is smart? You might also want to check out Koko, a gorilla who learned about 1000 signs and 2000 English words, reaching the level of a two to three-year-old human.

SOME INSIGHTS ABOUT INSIGHT

Cognitive psychologists also study how people solve problems. Problem solving involves mentally working to overcome obstacles that are in the way of reaching a goal. Some problems are clear-cut with a defined solution; for example, how to find the area of a square. But some are not well-defined. These problems, with no clear path to a solution, are also known as **insight** problems. Here is an example that was actually used in research: Two kids played five full games of checkers and each won an even number of games, with no ties, draws, or forfeits. How is that possible? There is no clear-cut way to solve this problem. It requires the ability to think in a creative, flexible way. Research shows that people are better able to solve these kinds of problems when they are in a good mood. If you spend some time thinking about the problem and you feel stuck, research suggests that you take a break. Other research shows that after a good night's sleep, people were more successful in solving insight problems.

By the way, if the insight hasn't struck yet: the two kids playing checkers were not playing against each other.

Check Out the Research

Liron Rozenkrantz and her team did a study to see if they could encourage people to think in more creative ways. They gave their participants something to smell. Half of the group just smelled it while the other half were told that the smell would increase their ability to think in clever ways. Then they gave a few tests, such as thinking of as many ways to use a common object as possible or extending squiggles into a picture. The people who thought the smell would make them more innovative thinkers performed better. This study showed that if you believe in your own powers of creative thought, you will perform in more original ways than if you doubt yourself.

? Did You Know?

Albert Einstein, the great physicist, used to take breaks to play his violin, which he found helped him to return to problems and think about them in new ways.

Try This

Gather six toothpicks. Now use those six toothpicks to make four triangles without breaking the toothpicks. (Hint: If you are stuck, gather some small marshmallows or little gumdrops. Does this help?)

Did you have a sudden ah-ha insight moment? What did you feel when that happened?

ARE COMPUTERS INTELLIGENT?

Computers can be programmed to perform human actions such as learning, problem-solving, decision-making, and language. Computers can win a chess game, compose music, answer questions, even drive cars. These are all examples of **artificial intelligence (AI)**. Cognitive psychologists use artificial intelligence to better understand human thought, and artificial intelligence uses findings from cognitive psychology. Today, scientists are working to create a computer system that can think creatively, and is not just programmed in a certain way. Would such an artificial brain be able to use insight and experience emotion? Psychologists are working alongside computer scientists to apply what they know about human thought to AI. One example is Psychlab, a simulated psychology laboratory that allows both humans and virtual subjects to participate in classic psychology experiments. This work is using cognitive psychology to propel AI forward. Now that's smart!

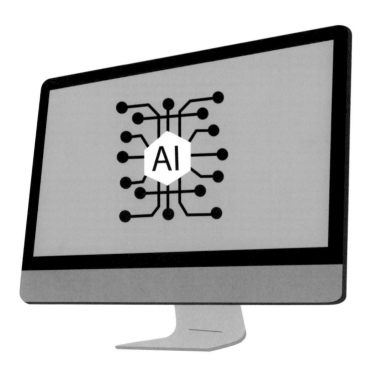

When you think about what it means to be smart, hopefully you will think more broadly than just school and grades. Different people have different smarts. You will think about people in other cultures who are smart in ways you may not have thought of before. And you will consider how language, insight, and problem-solving are uniquely human, even as computers are developed to become more like artificial brains.

NOW YOU KNOW!

○ Most intelligence tests today measure both crystallized and fluid intelligence.

○ The concept of intelligence is an umbrella over a wide range of cognitive functions. Intelligence tests produce IQ scores.

○ Intelligence tests have a useful role in the settings for which they were developed. IQ tests do a good job of predicting how well someone does in school, but they don't give us information about other important abilities. Motivation, training, and learning opportunities can have an impact on intelligence test results.

○ Theories of multiple intelligences go beyond a particular score on an intelligence test.

○ Animals can learn some language but human language, including sign language, is more complex.

○ Problems can have a clear path to a solution or require more insight and creativity.

○ Cognitive psychology is contributing to the development of artificial intelligence.

Chapter 9

HOW DO YOU REMEMBER?

Human memory is amazing! You can remember the words to a song, what you ate for dinner last night, how to add several numbers in your head, the rules of a game, the color of a jacket in a book illustration, that you need to bring a lunch tomorrow, and so much more. Just about everything you do involves memory. But how and why do you remember some things and forget others? And can you count on your memories being correct? What can you do to have a better memory?

TUNING OUT

You can't remember everything, and you wouldn't want to—you're experiencing too much! Before you can hang on to new information, your brain first sorts through your experience and only pays attention to some of it. You can't pay attention to everything at once, so in order to focus in on something important, you need to tune out other information. That's why it's not safe to walk and look at a cell phone at the same time. The more you focus on the phone, the more likely you are to trip.

Try This

Look carefully at the picture below. What do you see? If you'd like, you can write a list of all you see. Don't read the next section until you're pretty sure you noticed everything.

Now, cover the picture. What did you see and what did you miss?

- Seven monkeys?
- A guitar?
- A tire swing?
- A big ball?

Okay, let's try some harder things.

- A child eating cotton candy?
- A red dog collar?
- A trash can?
- A sign that pointed to the rest rooms?

It's impossible to notice and recall every detail! We all miss information, even when we think we're paying very close attention! How much you remember depends on the amount of information you pay attention to, but there's more to it than that.

Check Out the Research

In a famous experiment from 1999, Christopher Chabris and Daniel Simons made a video of two teams of people, one team in black shirts and one team in white shirts, passing a basketball. The scientists asked people to count the passes between only the people with white shirts. After the short video was finished, the researchers asked the participants to tell them how many passes they counted. But they weren't really interested in the number of passes. You see, half-way through the video, a person in a gorilla costume had walked across the court, right through the game. Half the people watching the video didn't even notice the gorilla! Even when we think we're paying careful attention to what we're looking at, we miss things, sometimes very big and surprising things!

Not only do we all miss many things that are right in front of us, we also can miss important changes that happen right before our eyes. Psychologists call this **change blindness**. This is what magicians rely on so that they can trick us. We may watch a magician make a coin disappear from his hand only to find it in someone's ear, completely missing how they did the trick.

Check Out the Research

Researchers Daniel Simons and Daniel Levin stopped people and asked for directions. While they were talking, two men carried a door between them, which allowed the person who had asked for directions to switch places with another person. Only half of the people giving directions noticed that they were now talking to someone else!

This cool study shows how our attention can be distracted away from details that seem obvious.

Can people fail to notice when the person they are speaking with changes? Check out YouTube videos of the "door study" by Simons and Levin where a door is passed between two strangers.

TUNING IN

Once your brain grabs onto information, it stores some of it for a very short time, less than a minute, in **short-term memory**. If someone tells you their phone number, but then you get interrupted, you probably won't remember the phone number. When you actively try to remember a phone number, you probably group the digits, such as the area code. If you are familiar with the area code, you probably don't think of it as separate digits, so it counts as one piece of information. You might notice other ways you can group the numbers. For example, if part of the phone number is in order, like 4 5 6, you can group that set of three and remember more easily. You can remember information more easily if it is grouped in some meaningful way. Grouping information to make it easier to store in short term memory is called **chunking**.

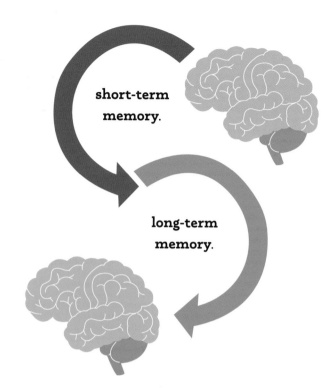

short-term memory.

long-term memory.

If you want to remember that phone number or another piece of information beyond short-term memory, your brain needs to perform some action to make sure the information moves into **long-term memory**. You might **rehearse** the information—that is, mentally review in some way, like repeating it over and over to yourself.

When you are learning information that you will be tested on, some of the most effective study strategies are testing yourself and explaining the material to yourself. The more you can connect new information with what you already know in this way, the more likely the material will stick in long-term memory.

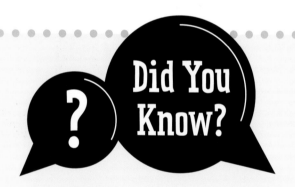

Did You Know?

?

3.1415 9265358 ...

Pi is defined as the distance around a circle divided by the distance across it. This number is constant no matter the size of the circle: it is always 3.14159265358979323846…the digits after the decimal point go on forever without repeating. Most people just use 3.14 for pi. But others are interested in how many digits after 3.14 they can memorize. The world record was set in 2015 by a man in India who recited pi to 70,000 decimal places! It took him ten hours. We don't know exactly how he did it, but he must have grouped the digits in a meaningful way so that he could remember them.

Try reading this set of letters to a friend or family member.

ugaotemcosd

Read the letters slowly and steadily. After you have read them, ask the person to tell you the same letters in order.

Now say that you will read another group of letters:

dogcatmouse

(the same letters as in the first group)

Read the letters slowly and steadily. After you have read them, ask the person to tell you the same letters in order.

If your participant recognized that the second set of letters contained words, then they probably found the second set of letters easier to remember because the words are familiar and already chunked into fewer units and stored in long-term memory.

YOUR BRAIN AS A CONTROL TOWER

Did you know that your brain can act like the control tower at an airport? Planes flying in and out need a central organizer to keep them where they need to be. The control tower needs to keep in mind the path of an incoming plane while at the same time directing a plane that is ready to take off.

Your **working memory** acts like a control tower, allowing you to remember some information while you are thinking about other information. For example, when you read a paragraph, you need to remember what you just read as you are taking in the rest of the paragraph. You have probably played math games at school where the teacher calls out a series of equations and you have to figure them out in your head. Working memory allows you to do that sort of mental gymnastics. Your short-term memory is a part of working memory, but working memory involves remembering something while also working on something else.

Try This

You use working memory with pictures. Ask a friend or family member to volunteer, and then have them look at this set of objects for 5 seconds:

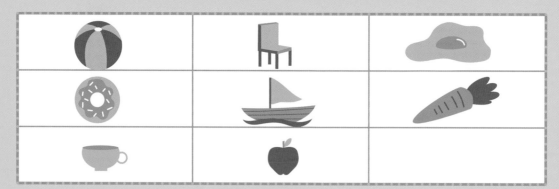

Now show them this set for 5 seconds:

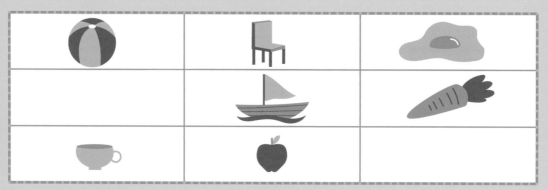

Using the empty boxes below, have your subject point to the spaces that were blank in the second set. Then ask them to identify whether the missing object was food.

People need to use working memory to do this quiz. They have to remember each item, where it's placed, and whether it's food. You certainly need a control tower to juggle all of that!

REMEMBER THAT?

If you want to remember something for a long time, you need a strategy to transfer it to **long-term memory**. Strategies like talking to yourself about what you are trying to learn, forming mental pictures of information, or organizing information into a brief, and possibly funny story can help.

Try This

Read through your family shopping list three times. Now ask a parent to check the list while you see how many items you can remember. The next time your family plans a trip to the store, read through the list but turn it into a silly story like:

"The smooth bald apples were jealous of the curly-headed broccoli. Then they realized that they could make themselves lovelier with earrings made from cherries and a fine necklace of peas. Alas, their new outfit was destined to be destroyed once the peanut butter and mayonnaise glopped onto the scene."

Now check your memory for this list. How did it compare?

FALSE MEMORIES

Imagine that you are in the lunch room at school. A kid you've never met comes to your table, picks up a bookbag, and leaves the room. There are kids on either side of you. Did you all see the same thing? Well, you did, but you probably won't describe what happened the same way. One of you might say the kid was wearing a blue sweater; the other might claim it was green. Was the kid wearing glasses? You might not have noticed. We can't pay attention to everything and so we don't always notice what is right in front of our eyes!

Sometimes we think we heard or saw something and we didn't. One of you might think the kid had a hat and the other one is pretty sure there was no hat. Our brains trick us into thinking we remember something that is not true!

The kid who comes into the lunch room either has a hat or doesn't. One person is remembering wrong. Researchers have shown that people often have false memories. The scientists read word lists to people similar to this one: sun, ocean, fish, sand, surf, swim, waves, dock, crab, boat. Then they waited five minutes and asked the participants to say the words they still remembered. Are you surprised that a lot of people said "beach" even though it wasn't on the list?

Check Out the Research

Elizabeth Loftus, a psychologist, is famous for her work that shows that people can be swayed to believe they observed behaviors that never happened. Her work has changed how we think about witnesses, especially in the courtroom. In one of her many experiments, Dr. Loftus and her colleagues showed people slides of a car stopped at a stop sign. Afterward, half of the participants read statements that the car had stopped at a yield sign (untrue) while the other half read true statements (that the car stopped at a stop sign). Then all the participants were tested on what they had seen on the slides. Participants who received false information were more likely to report incorrectly that the car had stopped at a yield sign. Memories can be affected by what people are told.

Since memory may be inaccurate, with people either missing or adding in details, Dr. Loftus's research affected how the police should talk to witnesses of a crime. It's important that when they are asking someone about what they saw they should ask in an open-ended way, "What was the person wearing?" and not make suggestions such as, "Was the suspect wearing a red shirt?" It's also important that witnesses be questioned separately so that they are not influenced by what others said they saw.

What you do and don't tune in to affects what you remember. And once you do tune in, you can improve your memory with strategies that help you store information as well as pull it out when you need it. But we're all human, and that means for most of us an imperfect, sometimes inaccurate memory.

NOW YOU KNOW!

○ Paying attention is tricky. We need to tune out some information to tune in to other information. No one can pay attention to everything!

○ Just like we can't pay attention to everything that we see and hear, we also sometimes make memory errors: we think we saw or heard something that we didn't. We also miss seeing things because our attention is turned elsewhere.

○ Your brain can only grab on to some of the information surrounding you to store in short-term memory. This storage is temporary. Information in short-term memory is either lost or moves on to long-term memory.

○ In order for information in short-term memory to move to long-term memory, your brain must perform some action so you can hold on to the information. There are several ways that this retention happens.

○ To keep information front and center in your mind right now, you need to mentally juggle it. This juggling of information is known as working memory.

○ When you memorize information, it moves to long-term memory. Testing yourself, explaining the material to yourself, and connecting information to what you already know are effective study strategies.

○ People may remember incorrectly, which is a problem for the police and the courts.

Chapter 10

HOW DO WE THINK?

What steps do you go through to make a decision or a judgment, or to answer a question, or to perform an action? You have to understand the task or question or problem, sort through your knowledge and memories, consider alternatives, put separate pieces of information together, and organize a response. It's a wonder you can accomplish anything!

TO THINK CAREFULLY OR NOT TO THINK CAREFULLY

When you first learned to ride a bike, each part of the procedure took your full concentration. Activities that you do in a careful, step by step way are called **controlled processes**. Controlled processes require effort and awareness. But a lot of what you do becomes automatic. **Automatic processes** require little effort or attention: you just do them. Once you learn to ride a bike, it becomes automatic. But if you are riding along and come to a bumpy or difficult section of the bike path, it will be necessary to use controlled processes again to get through

safely. Both controlled and automatic processes are helpful in different ways. When you pack up your backpack to go home from school, you probably do it mostly automatically, but if you don't use some controlled processes, you may forget to pack something that you don't use every day but need to bring home. Have you ever gotten something to drink from the refrigerator and started to put it back in the cupboard? If you stopped yourself, your controlled processes kicked in to help you pay attention. Automatic processes are important and necessary. The effort to pay attention to every little thing we do would be too much. But automatic processes are also subject to error. Psychologists are interested in how these two processes work together.

Try This

Observe controlled and automatic processes in yourself. First write your name as you usually do. You've written your name over and over, so it's automatic. Now turn the paper over and write your name backwards. For most people, that's a controlled process, because you have to concentrate on each letter.

Check Out the Research

In the 1930s, J. Ridley Stroop did some experiments about how getting two kinds of information at once can confuse thinking. He asked participants to read some color words printed in black ink: red, green, brown, blue, purple. Easy, right? When he printed the same words in the correct colors (red printed in red, green printed in green, and so forth), he found that people were able to read them quickly as well. But then he got tricky. He showed the same color words printed in the wrong color ink. For example, the word "blue" might be printed in green. He then asked people to name the colors again—sometimes he asked them to ignore the word and read the color, and sometimes he asked them to ignore the color and read the word. Reading these mis-matched colors was a lot harder than reading the matched ones! The interference of color and word became known as the **Stroop effect**. One way of thinking about these experiments is that we do some tasks automatically, but the mismatch in color and word causes us to slow down and do the task in a more controlled way.

BLUE	ORANGE
GREEN	BLUE
YELLOW	GREEN
ORANGE	YELLOW
BLUE	ORANGE
GREEN	BLUE
YELLOW	GREEN
ORANGE	YELLOW
BLUE	ORANGE
GREEN	BLUE
YELLOW	GREEN

Explore Further

Look for an interactive online Stroop Test and try it for yourself. Keep track of your times. If you practice saying the color and ignoring the word, do you get faster? If so, you are working toward making a new skill more automatic. That is what practice is—it's getting more automatic at something.

We have a lot of information that is outside of our immediate awareness. Such **preconscious information** is available to us when we need it. For example, you are not always thinking about your arm, but now that you read the first part of the sentence, you may indeed be thinking about and sensing your arm. Psychologists study preconscious processes through **priming.** Priming is like a hint that you aren't really aware of. For example, say a friend told you they saw palm trees on vacation. Later, you hear the word *palm*. You are more likely to think of a palm tree than of the palm of a hand. Priming occurs even when the person never becomes aware of it. Catherine Deeprose's research team presented patients with recorded lists of words while they were asleep during surgery. After they woke up, they did not know what words had been presented, but when they were given the beginnings of words, they were more likely to finish the words with those that had been played through earphones while they were asleep. The mind takes in information sometimes without our even knowing it.

GLASS, FLUTE, DRINK

Have you ever had a tip-of-the-tongue experience? That's when you feel certain that you know something but you can't think of it right then. This is an example of trying to pull preconscious information into conscious awareness. If someone gives you a clue, that's priming. Usually, with a clue, you'll know right away what you were trying to think of.

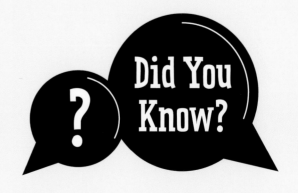

? Did You Know?

DECISIONS, DECISIONS

Every day, you make many decisions. Psychologists study how people decide, especially when those decisions don't make sense. Have you ever wanted to buy something because of the color even though it's more expensive? When people make decisions, there is often too much information to consider. So people take mental shortcuts, known as **heuristics**. In the 1950s, Herbert Simon described one heuristic, **satisficing** (a combination of satisfying and sufficing). He showed that people go through their choices one by one until they select an option that is just good enough. Satisficing can be a big help if you have to choose something in a hurry, such as picking a snack at the train station when the train is leaving soon.

You might say to yourself as you look at the rows of snacks: "No, not chips. That candy is too sticky. Hmm, cookies sound good. Those aren't my favorite kind but I'll take those." But even if you have more time, researching every option in order to make the so-called best possible choice actually does not make people happier. Good enough really is good enough.

Another commonly used heuristic is the **availability heuristic.** This mental shortcut happens when you base a decision or judgment on something that easily pops into mind. This heuristic can be useful. The last time it was cloudy and dark, it rained and you got drenched. So, when today it is cloudy and dark, your past experience pops into your mind, and you take your umbrella. But the availability heuristic can also fool us. For example, you look online and see vacation pics from some of your friends. Those pics fill your mind so you conclude that everyone went on an awesome spring break trip but you.

How do we make judgments? Amos Tversky and Daniel Kahneman in the 1970s showed that people tend to rely on how easily they can think of an example of something. For instance, in one study, they told the participants that they would be given several letters of the alphabet and asked to judge whether these letters appear more often at the beginning of words or more often in the third position in a word. A typical problem asked: Consider the letter R. Is R more likely to appear in the first position of a word or in the third position and how much more often? Participants were given five letters to judge. Overall, participants were far more likely to guess that the letters appeared in the first position and they guessed that the letters are in the first position twice as often as the third. But all the letters given actually appear in the third position more often. Why did people get this so wrong? The reason is that it is easier to think of words beginning with a given letter even though there are more words with the letter in the third position. People assume that what they easily think of happens more often. This thinking may lead to errors in judgment.

THINKING TRAPS

It is surprising how many different ways we get caught in thinking errors. For example, Aristotle, an ancient Greek philosopher, described a particular kind of reasoning called a **syllogism**, in which certain information is given and allows you to form a logical conclusion. Here's a present-day example:

All cars have wheels.
I am riding in a car.
Therefore, the car I am in has wheels.

This conclusion is true. The problem is that some apparent syllogisms can be false.

Here's an example:

All children like to play.
Dana likes to play.
Therefore, Dana is a child.

But Dana could be an adult, not a child.

How Do We Think?

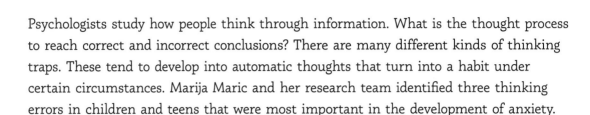

Psychologists study how people think through information. What is the thought process to reach correct and incorrect conclusions? There are many different kinds of thinking traps. These tend to develop into automatic thoughts that turn into a habit under certain circumstances. Marija Maric and her research team identified three thinking errors in children and teens that were most important in the development of anxiety.

MIND READING	
Assuming you know what someone else is thinking.	"Those kids are probably laughing at me." 
UNDERESTIMATION OF THE ABILITY TO COPE	
Thinking you won't be able to handle something.	 "I'll never be able to get used to a new school and make friends."
OVERGENERALIZING	
When one instance or example leads you to think it will last forever and will happen all the time.	"I got a C on my social studies test. I'm so stupid." 

These are examples of ways of thinking that have little to do with how smart we are and more to do with mental shortcuts that lead to exaggerated conclusions. Unless these sorts of conclusions are interrupted and corrected, we can start to believe negative thoughts about ourselves.

Another kind of thinking trap involves the human tendency to change what you think to feel better about something you've done. For example, suppose you buy a t-shirt from the school store. You then realize that you will not have enough money to buy the computer game you were saving up for. Your action (buying the t-shirt) is in conflict with your previous attitude (wanting the computer game). This sort of conflict between thought and action is called **cognitive dissonance**. Most often, people resolve the conflict—the dissonance—by changing the thought. For example: "I didn't really want that computer game." Cognitive dissonance was a theory proposed in 1957 by Leon Festinger. He and other psychologists did lots of research to prove that people fall into this thinking trap.

Check Out the Research

In a famous experiment, Leon Festinger and James Carlsmith gave students either $1 or $20 to tell another group of students that a very boring task was interesting. Afterwards, the researchers asked them how interesting they thought the task actually was. The people in the $1 group ended up reporting that the task was more interesting than did those in the $20 group. Being paid only $1 was not enough to justify lying, so the $1 participants experienced cognitive dissonance. They overcame the dissonance by believing the task was more fun and interesting than it was. There have been many studies since that show that people will change their attitudes in line with their behavior or change their behavior to match their beliefs, even if they don't realize they are.

Try This

Advertisements rely on cognitive dissonance. Right now, you are not buying their product because you feel you don't need it or it's not worth it. So, the advertiser needs to make you feel that you do need it and it is worth it. With these new beliefs, you are more likely to buy the item to bring your behavior in line with your thoughts. Write an ad for a new product of your choice that uses cognitive dissonance to get someone to buy the item. Here's an example: All the cool kids own a Jimper. You'll wonder how you ever lived without it. Get it at a new low price.

The more we understand about how people think and how the mind takes short cuts, the more we will be able guard against errors in judgment or negative thoughts about one's self. Psychology research is helping uncover how we think so we can think more clearly and make good choices in our behavior.

NOW YOU KNOW!

○ The mind is capable of different types of activity, which use different amounts of mental energy. Some are automatic, occurring without direct attention or effort, and some are controlled, using more immediate resources, attention, and thought.

○ When something is very familiar, it can be hard to process new information that conflicts with it.

○ The mind takes in information without awareness. We can't think about everything at once, so information is stored outside awareness but ready to call on when needed.

○ We use a variety of mental shortcuts to make decisions. Some decisions are good enough, but some are based on errors in judgment.

○ There are many kinds of thinking errors. Some are accepting false logic. Some are negative conclusions about oneself. Some are mental conflicts that we try to resolve, but not necessarily in a helpful way.

Chapter 11

HOW DO YOU CHANGE AS YOU GROW?

Do you ever look at pictures or videos of when you were a baby? It's amazing to think about all the changes you've gone through: from a tiny infant who couldn't hold up their own head to the strong, independent, clever you of today! And you still have so much growing ahead of you. What changes do all babies and kids around the globe go through? How does each one grow into a unique adult? Psychologists interested in child development ask and research these questions.

NEWBORNS DO MORE THAN SLEEP, CRY, AND LOOK CUTE

Although some people used to think that babies were born completely helpless and were shaped by the world around them, studies by psychologists have shown that babies actually have many abilities that make it easier for them to learn from their surroundings and to communicate with caregivers and others. In fact, one reason that babies cry is to tell those around them they need something. A baby's cry is hard to ignore, so caring adults quickly come to the rescue! In one study of mothers from around the world and their five-month-old babies, mothers responded to their baby's cry within five seconds on average, and tended to pick up the baby and hold or talk to them.

Of course, when studying babies, psychologists can't ask them about their experiences, so they have to find clever ways to figure out what's happening in their minds. For instance, they have used babies' facial expressions to learn what tastes they like. It turns out that babies are born liking the sweet taste of breast milk. That's not a bad survival plan! Luckily, for babies who may need a special kind of formula, they can make the adjustment. They may not like it at first, but they get used to it.

Even babies' sense of smell seems to help them out. It turns out that smell helps babies to bond to their caregivers!

Although a baby is born able to communicate by crying, it's important that they are also able to hear well in order to develop more advanced communication skills like talking. If you get your hearing checked, you can tell the person testing you when you hear a sound. But how do you tell if a baby is hearing? Researchers can test a newborn's hearing with equipment that measures whether their brain is reacting to sound. For babies who are a bit older, psychologists look to see if they move their heads or eyes towards a sound to check their hearing.

How do you tell what sounds a baby likes? Psychologists have found that they can connect a pacifier to a computer and see which sounds make the baby suck harder. Using techniques like this, psychologists have learned that babies know the difference between speech sounds and other sounds. Babies even recognize speech sounds that aren't used in the language their family speaks. They also like their caregivers' voices best and prefer when people use high pitched voices to speak to them. Research findings like these lead psychologists to believe that babies are born ready to learn language.

PEEK-A-BOO

Young babies can see faces and make out facial expressions, but only at very close distances. At birth, their ability to see color is not well-developed and things look a bit fuzzy, but babies start to be able to see more clearly within the first few months. As the eye muscles develop, babies get better at focusing on objects and seeing color. Once babies start to move around on their own, they learn a lot more about the visual world.

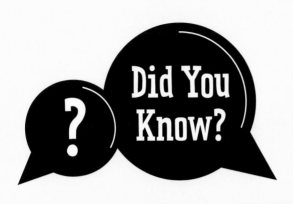

Did You Know?

Between birth and age two, the brain grows faster than any other body part. By age two, the brain is about 80% of its adult size. That's why early experiences are so important.

Check Out the Research

In 1960, Eleanor Gibson and Richard Walk created a box that had a steep cliff in the middle. Across the top of the whole box was a piece of glass, so you could crawl over the edge of the cliff safely—but it still *looked* like a cliff. The researchers called this a **visual cliff**. Babies were set down on the shallow side and encouraged by a parent to crawl across. Babies who had been crawling at home for a while stopped when they approached the part that appeared to have a drop-off. Babies who had only just begun crawling proceeded straight across. What did this visual cliff show? The researchers concluded that **depth perception** develops around the time babies start crawling. Later research showed that babies actually do see depth in the first three months, but only with crawling experience do they realize that a drop-off means a possible fall.

Explore Further

You can find videos online showing babies on the visual cliff. Check out Joseph Campos's research, where caregivers either smile or make a scared face as the baby approaches the drop-off. A smiling, encouraging caregiver could cancel out the child's natural caution and get them to crawl across! Why do you think babies were willing to crawl "off a cliff" if the caregiver signaled they should?

BORN TO LOVE

Young infants have just the right abilities to bond with their caregivers. In the late 1960s, a British psychologist, John Bowlby, described the close bond between parents or other caregivers and children. He said that the **attachment** bond affected kids in childhood and throughout their lives. Back then, parents didn't stay with kids who needed to spend time in a hospital. Bowlby saw that when parents left their children at the hospital, the children would become upset. He used the term **separation anxiety** to describe the fear that children experienced when apart from their parents. Bowlby's work was key in changing hospital rules so that primary caregivers could stay with their children. One member of his research team, Mary Ainsworth, developed a way to measure the parent–child bond in the lab, known as the **strange situation**. Her methods are still used in research today.

Check Out the Research

In 1970, Mary Ainsworth and Silvia Bell had mothers and one-year-olds come to a small room in the lab. There were three chairs, one heaped with toys, one for the mother, and one for a female stranger (one of the researchers). In the beginning, the baby was put down in the middle of the floor. The mother sat quietly unless the baby tried to get her attention. After three minutes, the stranger entered the room and sat quietly in her chair talking to the mother for a minute. Then she tried to interest the baby in a toy. As she did, the mother left the room. A few more brief separations and reunions followed.

What did the researchers make of all this coming and going? One of the key conclusions of this first study was that, in most cases, the baby was happy to play with the toys so long as the mother was in the room. The different ways that babies greeted the mothers after they returned to the room gave information about the parent-child bond. Most of the babies were considered **securely attached**, going over to their mothers immediately when they returned to the room. A small percentage that could not be consoled after the mother left were considered **resistant** and another small percentage ignored the mother and were considered **avoidant**. This research set the stage for later studies of how caregivers can help children to have healthy, secure relationships. Also, orphanages, adoption agencies, and hospitals now have policies based on helping infants to have a secure attachment with main caregivers.

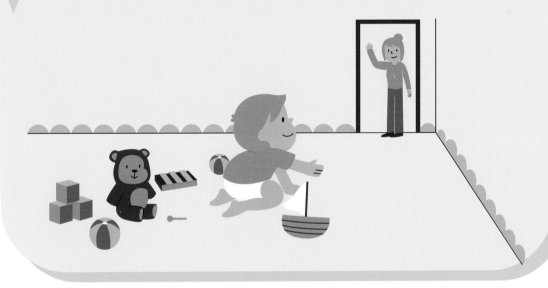

DIFFERENT FROM BIRTH

It seems that humans are born with a certain style of reacting to others and to their surroundings. From an early age, babies differ in their **temperament,** ranging from easygoing to fussy and difficult. When this was first studied in the 1970s, researchers relied on questionnaires completed by parents asking about how easily upset their infants were, how active and distractible, how regular in their routines, and so forth. Later, researchers developed other ways of studying how babies reacted in the lab or at home. For example, they would observe how easily babies became upset in reaction to unfamiliar sights and sounds.

Sometimes they also measured brain waves to look at the part of the brain that shows negative reactions. Studies using these various measures established that a baby's temperament tends to be about the same from the early months to the preschool years. About ten percent of infants responded strongly to noise and sound and were fussier than expected. This group was likely to become uncomfortable in unfamiliar settings as they grew through their preschool years. Luckily, adults and other kids can make a difference. Even a pretty jumpy, excitable, or easily upset kid can learn to stay calm and get along well.

Try This

Check with your parents or other caregivers to find out what you were like as a baby. How active were you? How much did you cry? How did you react to new people? What sorts of situations made you frustrated? How easily did you adapt to change? If videos of you as a baby are available for you to watch, what do you notice about your temperament?

THINKING IN INFANCY AND CHILDHOOD

A French psychologist, Jean Piaget, in the 1960s, observed his own children to see what he could tell about their thinking and knowledge. He used these observations to describe changes in how kids think as they grow. One of the most interesting parts of his theories explains how babies and children use and understand objects. Early on, infants tend to repeat behaviors using their own bodies such as sucking fingers or kicking a leg. Then they move on to using objects, such as banging a cup. By one year, they are very interested in objects. They can even pull on a blanket to help them reach a toy that is too far away.

In his experiments, Piaget found that, at about eight to nine months of age, babies appeared to understand that if an object was hidden from view (say by putting a blanket over it) it didn't mean it had disappeared. He referred to this awareness as **object permanence.** Although later psychologists have found that babies as young as four months old develop object permanence, Piaget was correct that infants go from not realizing an object still exists when they watch it being hidden to recognizing an object's continued existence even when out of sight.

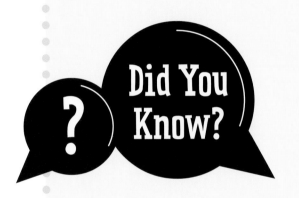

Around the world, adults and babies play peekaboo. One reason is that babies are surprised when you come back into view! As they get older, babies enjoy predicting the return of the hidden face. Eventually, they want to be the one to hide their face. Playing peekaboo with babies of different ages shows the development of object permanence in action.

Another famous psychologist, Lev Vygotsky, emphasized the social world of the developing child. Research based on Vygotsky's theories has looked at when young children recognize what other people might be thinking or feeling—this ability is known as **theory of mind.** A three-year-old thinks that everybody thinks like they do. By four or five, children realize that others may think differently. This development provides a basis for being able to think about one's own thinking and for identifying another person's thoughts and feelings. This is the beginning of **empathy.**

Try This

This is an experiment you can do if you know a three-year-old and a four or five-year-old (and have their caregiver's permission). It is known as a **false belief task**. Prepare your experiment by emptying a small box of crayons and replacing them with some candles. Then ask the child what they think is in the box. Of course, they will say crayons because it is a crayon box. Now open the box and show them the candles. Then, ask what they think their mother, father, or another person will think is in the box. A three-year-old will say candles. They saw the candles you showed them and they think everyone will know there are candles. A four to five-year-old child will understand that another person will have no way to know you made a change, and will say crayons. If you don't know any young children, you can find videos of this sort of task online.

It's amazing how much children master from birth through the preschool years, preparing them for the important learning years ahead. As kids enter school, they already know a lot about how the physical world works, about language, and about other people. Each stage of development builds on the previous ones as kids learn about themselves and the world around them.

NOW YOU KNOW

- Psychologists use a variety of methods to understand infants' basic senses and show how those senses help them bond to their caregivers.

- Skills and abilities develop together. For example, the ability to see a place where one might fall depends on experience with moving around.

- Children form bonds with caregivers that help them feel secure when they are nearby and cause anxiety when they are separated.

- We come into the world with differences in how easygoing we are. A difficult temperament might make early experiences tougher, but parents and teachers can help kids be more comfortable.

- Through infancy and childhood, we gain thinking skills that allow recognition that an object no longer in view still exists and recognition that others have their own thoughts and feelings.

Part 5

UNDERSTANDING FEELINGS

Chapter 12

HOW DO YOU FEEL?

You just found out that your very close friend is moving far away. You feel_____.

You would probably say "sad." Sad is an emotion, but what does it mean to be sad? When you are sad, you know it. You may get certain feelings in your body. Maybe your throat gets tight or your stomach hurts. You likely frown. If you're really sad, you may start to cry. You might think of all the fun times the two of you had together and how you will miss your friend. Feelings are complicated and made of different parts, including awareness that something of importance has happened, physical changes in your body, and thoughts about what happened and what it means.

ARE EMOTIONS THE SAME EVERYWHERE?

At first, psychologists thought that people developed emotions through experience. If this hypothesis were true, we would expect that people in some cultures might have different emotions than we do because their experiences are different. But it seems that isn't the case. People from around the world can easily label emotions on the faces of others from very different cultures and ethnic groups. And physical reactions to emotions are universal as well. Some psychologists have questioned whether facial expressions of emotion (like a smile) are indeed universal, but research strongly supports the idea that those expressions—and our emotions themselves—are based in human biology.

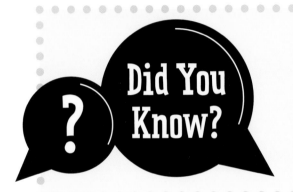

Did You Know?

Human faces have 43 different muscles that can be moved in thousands of complex combinations to communicate emotions to others.

Check Out the Research

A psychologist, Paul Ekman, and his colleagues made detailed maps of the many facial muscles used to express different emotions. Then they went to a very isolated spot in New Guinea where people had little contact with outsiders and no TV or movies (this was before the internet). The researchers made films of the people there. When they analyzed their expressions, they found they moved their faces just like Americans did to express emotion. People from very different cultures, who had no contact with one another, used the same facial muscles in the same ways to express emotions.

HOW MANY EMOTIONS ARE THERE?

Psychologists have debated how many basic emotions there are. Paul Ekman's research suggested that there are at least six: sadness, fear, anger, disgust, surprise, and happiness.

Later, he added embarrassment, excitement, contempt, shame, pride, satisfaction, and amusement to the list. But the evidence that these additional emotions are universal is less clear.

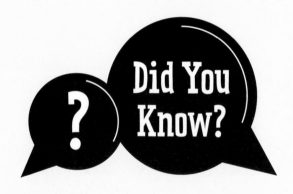

People cry for a number of different reasons and, it turns out, their tears reflect this. Different kinds of tears (sad tears, happy tears, or tears from cutting an onion) contain different molecules, and when you look at them under a microscope, they look different.

Another psychologist, Robert Plutchik, suggested a wheel of eight basic emotions, which he arranged on what looked like a color wheel. Blended together, these eight could combine to describe more specific emotions. Look up his wheel of emotions to learn more about his theory.

Explore Further

Understanding Feelings

HOW CAN I STOP NEGATIVE EMOTIONS?

Many people divide emotions into positive and negative emotions. What they're really getting at is that some emotions feel good (like happiness) and others feel bad (like sadness). While we might not like how we feel all of the time, and some emotions can present real challenges, we need all of them. We can think of emotions as an important signaling system. They give us a quick sense of what's out in the world that we need to protect ourselves from (fear), prepare to defend against (anger), avoid (disgust), pay attention to (surprise), or seek more of (happiness). If we didn't have those so-called negative emotions, we could end up in a lot of trouble!

The experience of disgust helped keep early humans from eating things that might sicken or even kill them. While the food you are likely to encounter now is usually safe, those ancient reactions to smelly or ugly foods still set off warning alarms.

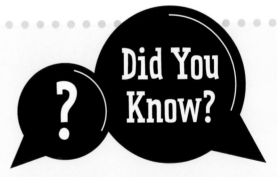

? Did You Know?

I GOT THE MESSAGE, NOW I'VE GOT THE SHIVERS!

Of course, you don't just read these emotional signals like a traffic light. Your body reacts to them—sometimes intensely! Some physical reactions are quite clear: you laugh or smile if something makes you happy, you jump if you're surprised, you get red in the face if you're angry.

In addition to what you are aware of, your body goes through some quieter internal changes when emotions are aroused. When you are afraid, your heart beats faster, your arteries get wider, you breathe faster, the pupils of your eyes expand, your liver releases sugar into your blood stream, and you start making more red blood cells. We call this the **fight or flight response** because that's what your body is getting ready to do in the face of danger!

Readying for fight or flight

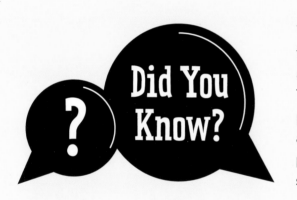

Did You Know?

Why do we call feelings "feelings"? You're probably familiar with the expression, "you hurt my feelings" and have heard people talk about "gut feelings." Those expressions seem to be talking about physical experiences but are meant to describe a mental state. The link between emotions and physical pain is strong. In fact, both activate the same areas and structures in the brain.

READING THE BOOK OF EMOTIONS

How can you tell someone else's emotional reaction? How do you express yours to others? Of course, sometimes people use language to tell others about their feelings. But even babies who can't talk are very good at letting you know when they're upset, happy, or frustrated. You can "read" emotions by observing how a person looks and acts. These signs are called **nonverbal cues**.

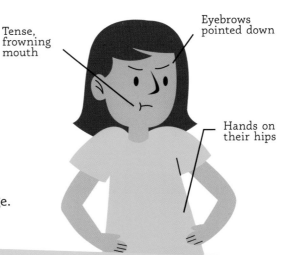

Tense, frowning mouth

Eyebrows pointed down

Hands on their hips

If someone looks like this person to the right, most people know that person is angry without any words. You can understand this by looking at their facial expressions and body language.

Check Out the Research

Until very recently, psychologists thought that you could spot someone who was lying by looking at their eye movements or body language. But research suggests those cues aren't very reliable. Recent research by Caso and Palena found that a story changing when a person tells it again is more reliable evidence that someone is lying. If someone can't keep the details of their story straight, they just might be making it up. So, paying close attention to what someone says may help you spot a lie more effectively than reading nonverbal cues.

Try This

If you want to check if someone is lying, ask them to repeat their story backwards. Do the details change? If so, it could be that the added effort of reversing what they made up is making it difficult to keep track of small specifics.

A funny joke can make you smile, right? First the joke, then the "hahaha!" Well, an interesting research study, by psychologists Fritz Strack, Leonard Martin, and Sabine Stepper, found that if you're smiling already, a joke is more likely to seem funny. They studied this by having people hold a pencil in their teeth (which put their mouth in a smile position) or between closed lips (which felt kind of like frowning). They were then shown the same cartoon. It turned out that the way their mouth was set changed how funny they thought the cartoon was.

What's so funny about that?

This guy is hysterical.

CAN YOU CATCH ANOTHER PERSON'S EMOTIONS?

You might be surprised to learn that the answer is, yes! Some researchers have found that when you recognize another person's nonverbal cues, you automatically copy them without even realizing it in a process called **autonomic mimicry**, also known as mirroring. And, once you make that facial expression, the emotion is likely to follow. That's how autonomic mimicry leads us to feel empathy for other people.

Try This

Try increasing how often and how long you smile at people. Do they smile back? Do you think they find your jokes funnier? Does it make it more fun to be with each other?

IF YOU'RE HAPPY AND YOU KNOW IT, CLAP YOUR HANDS

Imagine if you saw someone high up on a very narrow space in danger of falling. Your heart would start to pound, and you would start breathing faster. Your fear would alert you to do something NOW!

But how you understand what emotional signals and physical reactions mean has a big impact on your feelings. Going back to the example of a person at risk of falling: if you were at the circus and saw a tightrope walker, your eyes would send that information to your brain, which would put your body on alert, but because you understand the situation as entertainment, you would feel excited and happy and maybe move to a spot where you could have the best view. You would clap your hands rather than call for help.

Consider horror movies or haunted houses. Why would anyone choose to participate in something that scares them? Well, because we mix our emotions of fear and excitement and label it all together as fun! And, we also find it incredibly rewarding when we realize we're okay after being threatened by ghosts, monsters, or criminals!

THINK ABOUT IT

If the way you think about an experience leads to how you feel about it, does that mean that your thoughts can influence your feelings? The answer is yes!

When your first reaction is more angry or worried than is helpful, or when you're not as happy as you could be, it can help to have time for thoughts to jump in and make sense of the situation.

HEY!

For example, if a classmate grabbed your notebook and ran away with it, your quick signal system might trigger surprise and anger. But after a moment, when you see they are laughing and other friends are too, you might think, "they're playing around!" You might still be a bit annoyed, but probably not super angry. You might even laugh!

Sometimes people can get in the habit of having a lot of unhelpful thoughts. Those thoughts are automatic and built on past memories and experiences, but if you can alter the way you understand those past experiences, it can change our present reactions. If you find yourself having unhelpful thoughts, you can challenge those thoughts and try on less distressing ones. While changing thoughts isn't easy and takes practice, the goal is to trade unreasonable thoughts for more reasonable and accurate ones.

We all have emotions, but our thoughts about them can result in very different feelings. And that can lead to very different reactions.

Try This

The next time you start to feel extremely angry, try challenging your angry thoughts.

Is this important?

Could I be overreacting?

Don't do something you'll regret.

Step back and cool off.

Research indicates that people all over the world experience the same basic emotions. They play an important role in helping you to understand your experiences and the other people in your life. Emotions are closely tied to feelings in your body and to your thoughts.

NOW YOU KNOW!

- Research shows that all humans have the same basic emotions.

- Emotions we sometimes think of as "negative" (anger, sadness, fear, and disgust) are actually important to our safety and well-being.

- We tend to copy other people's emotional expressions without realizing it. This mirroring helps us to feel empathy towards them.

- Emotions and our bodies are tightly linked. Our bodies respond to emotions and we can alter how we feel about something by creating changes in our bodies.

- Thoughts and feelings are also closely connected. Emotions trigger thoughts as we try to determine what is happening around us and how to react. How we think about an event can also alter how we feel about it.

Chapter 13

WHAT MOTIVATES YOU?

You go to school each school day and do your work. When it's time for a test, you study for it and try your best to do well. Why? Maybe you enjoy learning and like to see some evidence that you are increasing your knowledge. Or maybe you like making your teacher and parents proud. Or maybe you feel competition with your classmates. Or maybe you feel a bit of all of these.

When you really want to do something for its own sake, we say you are **intrinsically motivated.** But sometimes we are driven to act by getting a reward or to please a parent or teacher, or to avoid a punishment or bad outcome. We call those sorts of drives or needs **extrinsic motives**.

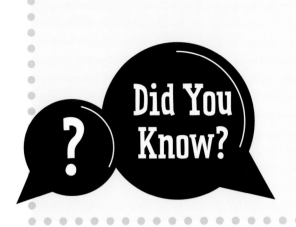
New brain research shows that your brain chemistry actually changes just thinking a behavior will lead to a positive result, which itself causes you to feel even more motivated to follow through. Expecting an activity to be rewarding adds to your motivation.

YOU'RE SUCH AN ANIMAL

There are many different kinds of intrinsic motivation. People are mammals and share many of the same **biological motives** as other animals. When those needs aren't met, your body sends signals to your brain that trigger you to do something about it. If you haven't eaten in a while, you feel hunger. If your body doesn't have enough water, you get thirsty. These motivators push you to act. Other biological needs, such as the need for rest and the need to avoid extreme cold, motivate you toward behaviors such as seeking a quiet shelter to sleep and stay warm. These basic needs, important to your very survival, are strong motivators.

FOR THE FUN OF IT

Of course, people are intrinsically motivated by more than biological needs. The desires to have new experiences and to have fun are also strong motivators. **Psychological motives** include the need for just enough, but not too much, excitement. We all need to have some new and interesting experiences. If nothing new ever happens, you get bored and will seek out ways to entertain yourself. But when you have too much stimulation, it can feel overwhelming and you will want to tone things down or withdraw.

PEOPLE NEED PEOPLE

We all have a strong need to have regular contact with other people. Psychologists call this a need for **affiliation**. If you don't feel you belong to a group or spend too much time alone, loneliness may set in and you'll feel a push to find other people to be with. It has been suggested that the need for others developed because early humans were better at finding food and staying safe if they were in groups. Others think this need is learned through positive experiences with parents and other people when we're really young.

Check Out the Research

One theory of why humans feel a need to be part of a group is for safety. In the late 1950s Stanley Schacter did a number of experiments to test this. In one he took two groups of college students and said they would be getting electric shocks. One group was told the shocks would tickle, the other that they would hurt. They then got to choose whether to wait alone or with other participants. The scarier description resulted in more research participants choosing to wait with the group.

People tend to be highly motivated by what friends and family think is important and interesting. If your friends think it's cool to do a volunteer project, learn skateboarding tricks, or read a certain book series, chances are more likely that you will want to do it also. This increased motivation through observation of others is called **motivational contagion**.

I CAN DO IT!

Achievement motivation is yet another kind of push to action. When psychologists talk about achievement in this context, they are considering things like doing well in school, but also other successes. A little kid's desire to brush their teeth "all by myself" is an example of achievement motivation. So is learning to play a musical instrument, learning to speak a foreign language, and baking brownies without adult help. Sometimes this drive comes from within a person, sometimes it comes from trying to please others, and often from some of both.

FIRST YOU GOTTA EAT!

Not everyone is motivated in the same way by the same things, and what a person finds motivating changes over time and across situations. In the 1940's a highly influential psychologist named Abraham Maslow hypothesized that some needs were more basic than others. A person would be more driven to find food than impress other people if they were starving. In general, he proposed that biological motivators come first, but once those needs are met, people would be motivated by less basic needs, like the need for creativity, being with and helping others, and other fulfilling activities.

Maslow's famous model can help us think about different types of motivations, though his thoughts about which were more or less important haven't been supported by research. Life turns out to be more complicated! We often have to deal with motives that:

Look up Lin-Manuel Miranda. What can you learn about the struggles he had before his big success with the show Hamilton? Can you identify achievement motives and psychological motives that impacted him? What biological motives might have pushed him on? Which extrinsic motives kept him working? What intrinsic ones?

Try This

When you're having difficulty getting motivated, think about what other needs may be distracting you? It's hard to concentrate on even the most enjoyable activity if you're very hungry or thirsty...or if you need to pee! Do you need to take care of biological needs first?

Needs for affiliation can sometimes interfere with other motives. If you're doing homework on a computer, even if doing well at schoolwork is important to you, it can be really hard to avoid being distracted by messages from friends. Even before computers, when your grandparents were kids, it was hard for kids to practice skills or read if they heard their friends playing outside. One way to handle these conflicting motives is to make sure you have time for both activities separately. See if you can set a certain time to meet friends online or in person to play or hang out. You may find yourself less pulled away from working towards other goals.

THE INS AND OUTS OF MOTIVATION

The interaction between intrinsic and extrinsic motives can be complicated and result in some surprising effects on behavior. For example, if someone loves to draw (is intrinsically motivated), they may actually stop drawing for pleasure if you pay them to do it (extrinsically motivate them) and then stop the payments. The same weird effect can happen with punishments for things you want people not to do.

Check Out the Research

A study by Samuel Bowles in Israeli daycare centers suggested that making people pay fines can backfire. First, he looked at how often parents were late picking up their kids when they got no penalty. Then, the center started charging parents for being late and they had even more of a problem with parents not getting there on time. Parents didn't see the fine as a punishment. Instead they just saw it as something else to pay for, and decided it was worth it!

Of course, extrinsic rewards, like an allowance or an earned treat, can be highly motivating. They just may not be as effective if you don't need that extra reason to do something. And extrinsic penalties may work if they make a less desirable behavior seem too "costly."

MOTIVATION AND LEARNING

Does motivating students with a reward help them to learn? Research by Kuo Murayama and Andrew Elliot found that it depends on how you measure learning. Studies conducted both in a laboratory and in a school setting suggested that how a person thinks about a goal affects learning. Individuals who are motivated by thoughts of doing well in the short run (such as getting a good grade on a test) may reach that immediate goal but improvement may be temporary. On the other hand, if a person is motivated to master a skill out of interest (like improving their ability to do math because they are interested in the subject), improvements can last for years.

I'M GOING TO BEAT YOU!

We often think of competition as motivating people. An elite athlete trains for hours every day in hopes of being an Olympic gold medalist. A student does research and spends time devising an outstanding project that just might win recognition at a science fair. But it turns out that the effect of competition isn't consistent, because competition can focus on either **approach** or **avoidance goals**. When a person is focused on doing better than others, they will be motivated to work toward a goal (an approach motivation). But people can also be motivated by not wanting to do worse than others (an avoidance motivation). Approach goals tend to be more successful than avoidance goals.

WHAT IF YOU JUST DON'T FEEL LIKE IT?

Are there times when you want to do something but feel like you just can't make yourself do it? Have you ever had trouble getting started? Do you sometimes spend time feeling bad about not doing something rather than just doing it?

I want to! I know it will be a good thing...maybe another day!

Setting and following through on goals is called **self-motivation**. Although we may be impacted by forces outside of ourselves, this kind of motivation comes from inside. It's an intrinsic form of motivation.

Sometimes, though, even someone who wants to follow through on a plan has trouble doing it. Psychologist Scott Geller, drawing on the work of Albert Bandura, talks about the four Cs of self-motivation:

- *Consequences*: the goal is important to the person.

- *Competence*: the individual feels they are able to do the action, it's important to them, and it's worth the effort.

- *Choice:* the person feels they have control over their actions.

- *Community*: Other people form a community that supports the person in trying to achieve their goal.

Try This

Can you use Geller's four Cs to motivate yourself? Pick something you'd like to learn or do more of.

- Consequences: Write your goal on a piece of paper or in a journal. Why do you want to achieve this goal? What will it mean to you if you can do it?

- Competence: Ask yourself whether you have the skills, time, and resources to go after your goal. Does it seem important enough to you to put effort into it? If not, can you think of an easier goal that might be a step toward a big goal?

- Choice: Do you have enough control over actions that could lead to your reaching your goal? Does it require money, transportation, or decision-making that require adult help? If you can't do it alone, see step 4.

- Community: Who will cheer you on, share your success, and support you in your efforts? If you need adult permission, financial backing, rides, and such, have you reached out to parents or other adults, and are they in your corner?

If you've thought through the four C's, you're ready to make a plan for how to take at least a baby step toward that goal each day (or each week). At the end of the day, write down whether you followed through. If yes, take a minute to feel good about it!

Motivation comes from both within and outside of us. Motivations come from a number of different sources and sometimes conflict with one another. Someone might be motivated to read a chapter of a book every night but not get around to it because of a competing motivation to stay in touch with friends online. Knowing more about how motivation works can help us to understand how to more easily achieve important goals.

NOW YOU KNOW!

○ The drive to do something is called a motive.

○ Motives can come from a desire to do something (an intrinsic motive) or from rewards and pressures from others (extrinsic motives).

○ Intrinsic psychological motives (like the need to do interesting things and have new experiences), affiliation motives (the need to be with others), and achievement motives (the desire to learn and get good at things) are universal. People can differ a lot, however, in how important those things are to them.

○ Some motives just demand to be dealt with before others. This is especially true of biological needs.

○ Motivation based on achieving a skill can be more effective for long-term learning than motivation to do well on a test or other performance in the short term.

○ The impact of competition on motivation is complicated since competition may involve approach or avoidance goals or both.

○ Thinking about what is (or isn't) motivating you and focusing on additional motives can be helpful when you just can't seem to get yourself to do things you want or need to do.

Part 6

CARING FOR YOURSELF

Chapter 14

WHAT IS STRESS?

"I'm really stressed out." You hear people say this, but what does it actually mean? **Stress** is an event or circumstance that strains a person's ability to manage. Quite a wide range of stressors (sources of stress) can produce a reaction. A stressor can occur once, happen repeatedly, or be present in an ongoing way. It can be routine, like a tough exam; caused by a change, like parents divorcing; or be traumatic, like a major accident. Even positive events cause stress, such as a new sibling at home or starting a new, unfamiliar activity. Both the brain and the body respond to stress. And those reactions serve a purpose.

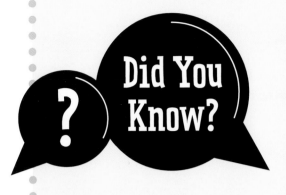
Many people say they are "stressed" when they really mean that they are feeling anxious. Stress occurs when something has happened or is happening that you are reacting to. Stress is external. Anxiety is a worry that something bad will happen. There is no obvious, immediate threat. Anxiety is internal. Of course, if a person experiences stress, they may start to struggle with anxiety later if they worry about a bad event happening again.

MIND AND BODY ARE CONNECTED

One of the ways that researchers see how people respond to stress is to measure their **cortisol hormone,** a substance that the body releases in response to stress. The cortisol signals a fight-or-flight situation, but if cortisol remains high, it is harmful to the body. Psychologists can measure cortisol levels in saliva before and after activities to see if stress levels went down.

The ways in which stress can produce both a set of feelings (such as alarm or a feeling of pressure) as well as have an impact on the body (rapid breathing and muscle tension for example) demonstrates a **mind-body connection**. The brain, via thoughts and feelings, influences the body and its functions. The health of the mind affects the health of the body.

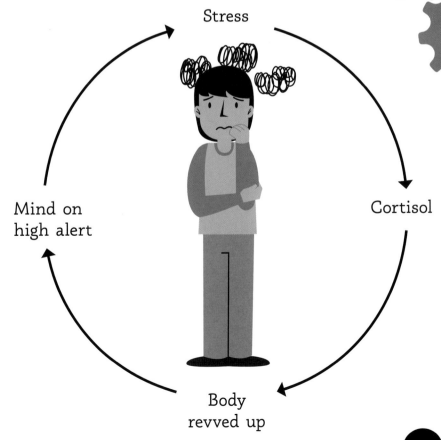

Stress

Cortisol

Body revved up

Mind on high alert

STRESS CAN BE UNHEALTHY...OR GOOD

When a danger is real but brief (like a strong thunderstorm) the stress reaction is a useful alerting system that passes quickly once the threat is avoided (you go indoors to ride out the storm). But when stress sticks around, fight-or-flight reactions can be hard on the body and on the emotions. Those very life-saving changes in the body that signal danger can impair health if the stress is either huge and traumatic, like war or a destructive hurricane, or continuing, like poverty, illness, or emotional challenges. Even things like too much pressure from adults to perform at a high level or being in a class that's too difficult can create a hurtful stress reaction in your body. People who have experienced long-term and/or intense stress may suffer headaches, stomach aches, and other physical problems.

But not all stress is bad. Stress can also be energizing and get you moving. Think of your team before a swim meet. The tension you feel in anticipation of competition is a kind of stress that will motivate you and your teammates to try for your best times. When stress is temporary, when the situation is safe, and when there's not too much of it, it can be useful and even desirable.

How you think about stress can affect how it impacts you. It turns out that if you believe stress is hurting you, it's more likely to do so. But if you take a more positive view and see stress as a useful challenge, you will have a more positive outcome. If you choose to welcome the helpful effects of stress, you may reduce the discomfort it causes.

Check Out the Research

Alia Crum and colleagues in a 2012 study introduced a stressful situation in a college classroom, suggesting that some students would need to give a presentation and receive feedback on their charm and appeal as speakers. Some of the students said stress is helpful and others said stress is hurtful. Students were assessed on several measures of stress in response to knowing they would have to complete the public speaking assignment. The students in the "stress is helpful" group actually experienced less stress than those in the "stress is hurtful" group.

One reason that it matters how you think about stress is that your outlook affects how you handle it. When you see yourself as able to handle stress, you are likely to problem solve, take action, and turn to others. In fact, stressful experiences can make you better able to bounce back from difficulty in the future.

Typical Stressors Reported by Kids

Exams

Difficult classes at school

Wanting to watch TV instead of doing a required task

Not liking a teacher

Having too many activities outside of school

Forgetting something important

Problems with friends or family members

Do any of these sound familiar? While none are traumatic or tragic, they can each cause a stress response to a varying degree.

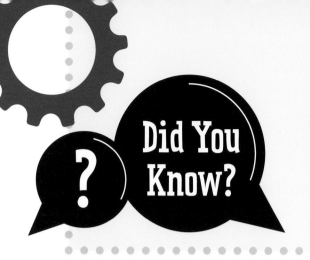

Did You Know?

According to a 2010 report by The American Psychological Association, up to half of children from ages 8 to 17 reported feeling worried and many reported headaches, sleep problems, and upset stomachs. Their stress caused considerable anxiety.

COPING WITH STRESS

Psychologists have learned a lot about stress by studying the everyday events that challenge people. How much stress kids experience depends in part on how they **cope**. Coping is what you do to manage difficulties. Lots of kids deal with stress by pushing it away, instead of talking about their experience or actively handling the stress. But pushing thoughts away doesn't work.

Check Out the Research

How easy is it to push away a thought? Daniel Wegner and his colleagues did several studies to learn about thought-stopping. In one, they asked college students to report all their thoughts for a five-minute period, trying not to think of a white bear. If they did think of a white bear, they were to ring a bell on the table in front of them. The task was basically impossible. Thoughts of white bears intruded.

While pushing away thoughts doesn't help, the coping strategies that work best are ones that help a person see themselves as able to cope; for example, "I tell myself I can handle this" or "I tell myself that I can learn from this situation" or the like. **Self-talk**, what you say to yourself, allows you to approach stress in a more positive way. When your fight-or-flight signal is making your body react, think about how your pounding heart and rapid breathing are giving you energy to handle the challenge.

CALMING THE MIND

One way to keep stress from interfering is to learn how to calm yourself. **Mindfulness** is essentially the opposite of blocking thoughts. Research shows that it works well to manage stress. Think about stressful thoughts as like a snow globe. When it's shaken, the snow is blowing around helter-skelter. But after a while, it settles down. Mindfulness is a way of getting thoughts to settle down.

Mindfulness can also direct us to be more attentive to others. An example is putting aside all electronics for a family dinner in which each person tells a joyful moment from the day. The family might take a quiet moment to focus on being grateful for being together. When distractions are reduced and busy thoughts quieted, people say they feel calmer and, therefore, less stressed.

Try This

Here's a mindfulness exercise called RAIN:

R   Recognize the feeling. Note what you are feeling.

A   Allow the experience to just be there. Whatever you are feeling is temporary. Just stay with it.

I   Investigate the feeling with kindness. Where are you tense or relaxed? What thoughts go with the feelings?

N   Non-identification. The feeling is not who you are. It will go away in time; you can let it go.

If you try RAIN when you are upset, you will understand how mindfulness is about managing stress: not suppressing feelings but not clinging to them either.

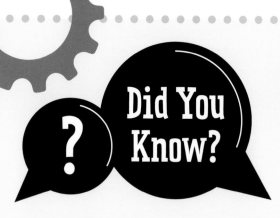

Baoding balls, likely created in the 14th century in China, are small metal balls. Used as a pair and held in one hand, it is thought that they reduced stress by stimulating certain points on the hand, according to traditional Chinese medicine. Baoding balls, now made with various materials, are still common in China.

LEARNING TO RELAX

What are effective coping strategies for stressful situations? General self-care is helpful, such as exercise, eating healthily, sleeping enough, and engaging in relaxing activities. Relaxing activities could include listening to music, hearing a story, laughter and humor, or anything you find enjoyable. **Social support**, when family and friends help you feel cared for, can help lower stress as well.

Check Out the Research

Research has shown some specific ways to manage stress before an exam. In 2019, Christopher Rozek and his colleagues published a study in which they had randomly assigned one of four tasks right before a science test. One group was told to ignore their feelings of stress. Another group was told to write about their stress for 10 minutes. The third group read about stress reactions, like sweaty palms, and how stress could be helpful before an exam. The last group did both the writing assignment as well as reading about stress. All three groups who actively faced the stress did equally well on the science test: kids who wrote about their stress, read about stress, or both all did better than the group who were told to ignore their stress.

Prepare yourself to handle stress by thinking of activities that help you relax ahead of time. Create four lists titled Move, Make, Chill, and Connect. Then add activities in each category that work for you. Under Move, include any physical movement that calms you. Under Make, include creative activities. Under Chill, include quieting activities. Finally, under Connect, include social activities. Here's an example:

MOVE	MAKE	CHILL	CONNECT
Take a walk	Draw	Read	Phone a friend
Dance	Cook	Take a warm bath	Attend a club event

The next time a stress occurs, go to your lists to select possible helpful activities.

A DOSE OF NATURE

Although avoidance doesn't work, taking a break from stressors helps people feel less overwhelmed. One arena for taking a break is getting out in nature. Research consistently shows the benefits of green spaces for reducing stress. You might wonder if it's the exercise that people tend to get when they are outdoors as opposed to the nature itself. But researchers Alan Ewert and Yun Chang published a study in 2018 that showed that visiting a forested area was more beneficial in lowering stress than visiting a city park or an indoor play or exercise area. It seems the more purely natural, the better.

There may be many reasons why being in nature helps people feel less stress. One possibility has to do with how you direct your attention. Generally, when outdoors in nature, your attention is captured but not intensely focused. The part of your brain that concentrates gets to relax and recover. A second feature of being in nature is a sense of escape, a break from stress. There appear to be some substitutes for being outdoors in nature. For example, truly amazing, awe-inspiring nature videos—the kind with beautiful panoramas of mountains, oceans and so forth—capture participants' attention so that they are focused outward and no longer as focused on themselves and their stressors. So if you can't get outdoors, experiences that fill you with wonder, as in watching spectacular scenery, are also stress-reducing.

Explore Further

Look up some awe-inspiring nature videos and see how you feel watching them. Do they capture your attention, get you out of yourself, and help you feel relaxed?

Try This

If you can't get out in nature, according to research, imagining yourself in nature can substitute. You can create your own scene or use this one:

Close your eyes. Imagine you are walking through a lovely magical forest. This forest is a safe and happy place. The sun is shining and you feel a gentle breeze. You hear the sounds of birds and see the beautiful trees gently swaying. Your path is lined with colorful flowers. On your walk, you come upon a patch of moss and sit down for a rest. The moss is soft and inviting. After a rest, you walk a bit further and see a burbling brook. Next to the brook is a pile of smooth stones. You enjoy tossing the stones in the brook and watching them splash. When you are ready, you continue your walk feeling calm and peaceful. As you exit the forest, you know you carry with you the sights and sounds and feel of this beautiful place.

We can't prevent many sources of stress, but the more psychologists research about stress, the more we learn how to help people during or after a major stressful event, as well as how everyone can better handle everyday hassles. When stress is handled well, the mind and the body feel better and stay healthier and you get tougher and learn how to bounce back more readily.

NOW YOU KNOW!

- Stress is an event or circumstance that strains a person's ability to manage. Stress can range from the disastrous (like a house fire) to positive changes (like starting middle school) to everyday hassles (like conflict with a friend).

- Typical responses to stress include emotional upset and physical symptoms such as headaches, stomach upset, and problems sleeping.

- Cortisol is released in the body when we feel stress, which in turn is part of a fight-or-flight response, and has an impact on both the brain, signaling there's an emergency, and on feelings, which are on high alert. This process is a connection between mind and body.

- When stress is temporary and not too intense, and the situation is safe, it can be motivating and useful.

- It is nearly impossible to tell yourself not to think about something, and avoidance does not work well to manage stress.

- Coping strategies are actions that help manage stress. One coping strategy, mindfulness, is a process of awareness and acceptance of the present situation. Other useful coping strategies include positive self-talk, general self-care, relaxation, accessing social support, written or spoken expression of concerns, and taking a break.

- One particularly effective way to take a break is to go out in nature.

Chapter 15

WHY DO YOU SPEND SO MUCH TIME SLEEPING?

People sleep a lot! Sleep experts say kids should sleep nine to ten hours a night and adults about eight. All those hours asleep every day might seem like a waste of time, but you need sleep for the health of your mind and body. Lack of sleep causes problems paying attention and difficulty learning, and interferes with your growth and fitness. The brain and the body recover from the day's activities during sleep, so not sleeping enough can interfere with your mood and your ability to cope. There's actually a lot going on when you sleep; you are not just lying there!

WHAT DO YOUR EYES HAVE TO DO WITH DREAMING?

During the stage of sleep in which you have most of your dreams, your eyes dart back and forth, your breathing becomes fast, and your heart rate increases. This stage is called **REM (Rapid Eye Movement)**. Even though your eyes are moving rapidly during REM, the rest of your body is especially still. Your arm and leg muscles actually become temporarily paralyzed, which prevents you from acting out your dreams.

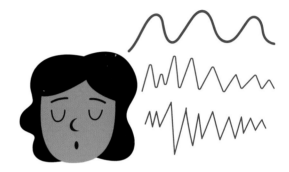

You may not remember what you dreamed by the time morning comes, but if someone wakes you up during a REM stage, you probably do recall what you were just dreaming. So, what are dreams and why do we dream? By using methods such as measuring brain waves, interrupting sleep, preventing sleep, and testing people, researchers now think that dreaming helps us store memories and separate them from intense emotions. So, dreaming lets us make sense of our daytime experiences and feel better about them. A dream state is a safer, calmer environment for remembering your day. Dream researcher Dr. Matthew Walker calls dreaming "emotional first aid."

Check Out the Research

Dreaming also increases flexible thinking and problem-solving. Matthew Walker and his research team study sleep and dreaming. In one study, they gave participants anagrams to solve—letters in a mixed-up order that you rearrange to form words, such as OSEOG = GOOSE. They had their research participants solve the anagram tests both when awake and when awoken from different sleep stages. They found that people did best when awoken from REM sleep. Several of the participants who were awoken from the dream stage of sleep reported that solutions "popped" into their heads. Those results, together with many other research findings, suggest that REM sleep and dreaming assist humans in flexible thinking.

Ask someone to close their eyes and move them. That is what people look like when they are in the REM stage. If possible, watch someone sleeping and see if you can spot REM sleep. But don't wake them up!

YOUR BUSY BRAIN DURING SLEEP

We know from studying brain waves that there are regular stages of sleep. When you first drift off to sleep, you are in Stage 1. This is a "light" stage in which you are pretty easy to wake up. In Stage 2, your heart rate falls and your body temperature drops. You are moving towards deeper sleep. In Stage 3, you are in a deep sleep. It is hard for someone to wake you during this stage. And this is the stage of sleep that helps you feel rested. Deep sleep allows your body to go through a process of growth and repair. Stages 1, 2, and 3 are called **Non-REM**. Most of the time, people don't dream in Stages 1-3. Stage 4 is REM sleep, where your eyes move rapidly and you have lower muscle tone.

We move in and out of the sleep stages like a roller coaster.

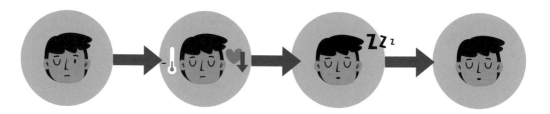

Each sleep cycle consists of the four sleep stages. People go through the cycle about four to six times a night, spending about 90 minutes in each cycle. Of course, sleep patterns change from infancy to old age. Babies spend about 16 hours per day asleep and about 50% of that time in REM sleep. Older people sleep about seven to eight hours per day and spend about 15% of that time in REM sleep.

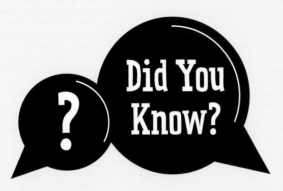

Sleepwalking is more common in children than adults, but overall, it's pretty unusual. When it does occur, it tends to happen in the early part of the night when someone is in Non-REM sleep. Typically, a child will sit up in bed with eyes open, although they are actually still asleep. They may wander from room to room, talk, even eat or get dressed. The main concern is safety, so the best response is to direct the person back to bed. If necessary, it's okay to wake someone while sleepwalking. Most people don't remember in the morning. Almost everyone outgrows sleepwalking and, in the meantime, it's important for those who sleepwalk not to sleep in a top bunk!

NIGHTMARES

Just about everybody knows what a nightmare is because just about everybody has had at least one frightening or unpleasant dream. Children tend to have nightmares more often than adults, probably because they are becoming aware of scary, worrisome, or difficult experiences for the first time. You now know that nightmares generally happen during the REM part of the sleep cycle because that's when dreams are most likely. If the nightmare is upsetting enough, you may wake up and remember what you just dreamt. Just like any dream, your mind is trying to deal with your emotions. In the case of nightmares, the emotions are intense and frightening. Nightmares can happen after you've experienced an actual scary event, seen a scary movie, watched

scary news, or imagined scary events. Or, they can happen out of the blue. Occasional nightmares are best dealt with by going back to sleep and thinking good thoughts, but sometimes nightmares get stuck and repeat. If you get stuck with the same nightmare over and over, try telling it with a new happy or funny ending the next morning.

Why Do You Spend So Much Time Sleeping? **163**

Check Out the Research

In 1992, Dr. Robert Kellner and his research team developed a way to stop nightmares that repeat. They called the method **imagery rehearsal therapy.** They had people write a new ending for the nightmare. It didn't matter what the new ending was as long as the person was satisfied with it. It could be happy, silly, funny, magical, or brave. Then they had people relax at home and read the new ending to themselves daily. Participants were able to greatly reduce how often they had nightmares and many got rid of the nightmares altogether.

Remember, it is basically a good thing that you dream, even if your dream is unpleasant. It is helping you overcome tough emotions and move forward.

BODY CLOCKS

Have you noticed that it can be harder to wake up for school after summer or winter vacations? Shifts in when you sleep can throw off your body clock. Our bodies don't have an actual clock inside, but the light and dark of the day signal a part of the brain that tells our bodies to wake or sleep. This day/night cycle is called **circadian rhythm.** If you pay attention to your body's cues, you will notice that you tend to get sleepy at about the same time each day. If you follow your circadian rhythm, your sleep will stay in balance, but a change in schedule can disrupt your body clock. Staying up late, sleeping late, and interrupted sleep can throw off your natural rhythm of wake/sleep. Also, the artificial blue light from electronics can confuse your body clock into thinking it's still day. Use of electronics can be hard to break away from, but if you use them too close to bedtime, you may ignore your body's cues and stay up later than you should.

A person's circadian rhythm changes as they go through puberty. People start not getting sleepy until later in the evening. As a result, it can be harder to get up early in the morning. For this reason, many scientists recommend that middle and high schools start school at 8:30 am or later.

Check out the Centers for Disease Control and Prevention (CDC) website for more information about later start times for schools.

Explore Further

Try This

Get in touch with your circadian rhythm by keeping some records of your sleep patterns. First, remove all electronics from your room (if you share a room, you will have to ask your family to help you with this experiment). Avoid using electronics one hour before bed. Instead, darken your room, using only low light. You can read or listen to soft music (turn all lights from any electronic device away from you). Pay attention to signals that your mind and body are getting ready for sleep. Estimate what time you fall asleep so you can record it in the morning. Notice what time you naturally wake up in the morning. (Ask a family member to be sure that you get up in time for school.) If someone needs to wake you, try moving your bedtime earlier until you are waking up on your own. When you wake up, get some exposure to light as soon as possible. Try to work toward a consistent bedtime and wake time. Take a look at the records you kept of your sleep and wake times. Were you able to take control of your personal circadian rhythm?

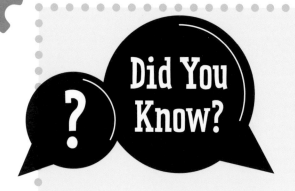

A giraffe only sleeps 1.9 hours a day on average, while bats sleep 19.9 hours. Animals also have circadian rhythms, influenced by the dark/light cycle. This is important in nature so animals can track the best times to hunt for food, stay safe, and when to migrate or hibernate.

DID YOU SLEEP WELL?

When people don't get enough sleep, they don't perform as well on tests of thinking. And while this finding is proven in many studies, it is also true that people's performances on thinking tests depend in part on their expectations. It turns out that how you think about your sleep can affect how well you do on tests. If you think you did not sleep well, even if you did, you might do worse on a test.

Check Out the Research

In 2014, Christina Draganich and Kristi Erdal published a study in which they gave people different fake information about their REM sleep to suggest that some participants had more than the usual percentage of REM while others had less than usual. They wanted people to believe they had slept particularly well or particularly poorly. First, they asked people how they felt they had slept, and then they hooked people up to a fake brain wave test and told them fake results. Actually, participants were assigned at random to the below average or above average sleep quality groups. Then they gave them a pretty challenging numbers test. You really had to be alert to get the test right! The experiment's results showed that people who believed they had poor quality sleep, even if they had reported that they thought they slept well, did less well on the test, as if they really hadn't slept well.

In general, it is a good idea to get enough sleep. But, if you don't get enough sleep one night, it might help to tell yourself that you're fine, or at least not tell yourself that you're too tired!

Sleep is a big and essential part of life. Researchers continue to study how our brains work while we sleep, how sleep helps us deal with emotions, how our bodies benefit from sleep, what we can do about sleep problems, and how we function based on our beliefs about our sleep.

NOW YOU KNOW!

- Most dreaming happens during a sleep stage called REM, Rapid Eye Movement.

- Dreaming helps us store memories apart from intense emotions and make sense of our daytime experiences and feel better about them.

- Stages 1, 2, and 3 of the sleep cycle are called Non-REM. We move through the sleep stages several times through the night.

- For bothersome nightmares, imagery rehearsal is effective. Change the ending of your nightmare and read it to yourself a few times.

- We have an internal circadian rhythm in response to light and dark that regulates sleep each 24-hour period.

- People can be tricked into believing they didn't sleep well—and believe it so much that they don't do as well on listening and thinking tests.

Part 7

TAMING EMOTIONS

Chapter 16

WHAT HELPS PEOPLE DO WELL?

What are the strengths that help people succeed? The field of **positive psychology** explores what produces satisfying and meaningful lives. Researchers study the role of positive emotions, individual strengths, positive relationships, and settings that promote well-being.

Taming Emotions

BE POSITIVE

If everything was always going well, what would you feel? Content, hopeful, happy, excited? These are positive emotions and they feel good! But there is more to having a good life than just feeling good. There's having strong interests and a sense of purpose, confident feelings about yourself, and connections to other people. These all are part of our well-being. But everything doesn't always go well. Positive psychology teaches you how to hold onto feelings of well-being even when you face challenges.

DEALING WITH FAILURE

It turns out that understanding what makes people happy is complicated. For example, if you feel that making the soccer team will make you happy, and you do make the team, then you will have positive feelings. If you don't make the team, what inner strengths and beliefs do you call on to stay positive? One answer is based on how you think about challenges. What is your **self-talk**, your inner conversation with yourself? If you think "I'm a failure," then you are likely to feel bad about yourself. Research by Martin Seligman and his colleagues showed that people can learn a different way of thinking that leads to feeling more optimistic and hopeful. For example, "I will practice my soccer skills more and try out again." To change unhelpful thoughts, it helps to be open about ways of thinking about yourself and others.

THINK. FEEL. ACT.

The study of how thoughts, feelings, and behaviors are connected and affect one another is based on **cognitive-behavioral principles**. Early theorists, such as Albert Ellis and Aaron Beck, realized that people who are depressed have a habit of thinking negatively that causes sad feelings and grumpy behaviors. They wondered if teaching people to think differently would make a difference in their feelings and behavior. Building on this concept, cognitive-behavioral principles emphasize how thoughts, feelings, and behavior affect each other. Any change in one of the three causes changes in the others. For example, if you think "I'm not good at art," you probably feel frustrated in art class and you may not put much effort into your work. If you think "Art is tough. I'm going to need some help from the teacher," you probably feel less frustrated and more hopeful and ready to work at learning art skills. This connection between thoughts, feelings, and behaviors leads to strategies to deal with everything from problems falling asleep, to fears, to anger, and even to depression.

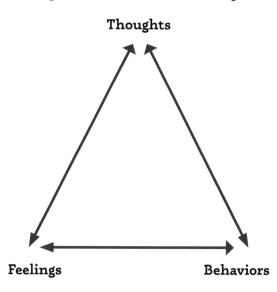

One common negative belief some people develop is that nothing they do matters. This thought leads to a feeling of helplessness and inaction. Researchers investigated how this cognitive-behavioral chain might work in animals and then in humans.

In the 1960s, psychologists Martin Seligman and Steven Maier did a series of studies using dogs. They compared the responses of dogs who were able to avoid an electric shock to those who had no way to avoid it. The group that learned to avoid the shock from the beginning did well and consistently avoided it. But when the other group later had a way to avoid the shock, they didn't use it. While this kind of experiment would not be approved today, the research became the basis for the concept of **learned helplessness**: the idea that when stress is beyond individuals' control, they act as if they are helpless even when they later have control. As further research was carried out, psychologists found that the amount of control one has affects well-being in humans as well.

Check Out the Research

In a later experiment by Donald Hiroto and Martin Seligman, people were placed in a room with a distracting noise. One group was shown how to turn off the noise and the other group had no control over the noise. Even though those who had a way to turn off the noise rarely actually did so, they performed better on written tasks than those without control over the noise. Being aware of one's control appeared to counteract the noise's disturbing presence.

IS YOUR GLASS HALF FULL OR HALF EMPTY?

Seligman observed that when people were presented with challenges, some didn't seem to believe they had control over the situation and gave up quickly. He wondered if this was a real-life example of learned helplessness. He was also interested in those who had a more hopeful outlook and kept trying in the face of failure. He suspected that people who viewed the world in a more positive way were protected from feeling out of control. As a result, he developed the concepts of **optimism** and **pessimism** as important to a person's functioning. Optimism is having a positive expectation for the future and pessimism is its opposite. Many studies have shown that by embracing optimistic thoughts and challenging pessimistic ones, people are better able to meet life's challenges.

Is it half full or half empty?

As the field of positive psychology has developed, optimism has been identified as one of several ingredients of well-being. Everybody's life has difficult events. Being able to adapt well in the face of challenges is called **resilience.**

When life throws a curveball, what do you do to come back strong? Research points to these basic characteristics of people who are resilient.

you know your strengths and weakness.

you have a positive sense of yourself.

you allow others to help you out.

You know you're resilient when...

you don't ignore your strong feelings.

you are open about ways of thinking about yourself and others.

you take action to solve problems.

you can stay cool and calm.

Try This

The Penn Resiliency Program developed this exercise to teach kids optimism: Every day for a week, write down three good things that happened. Next to each positive event, write down why this good thing happened, what it means to you, and how can you have more of this good thing in the future. Most people find this exercise helpful.

"My friend and I ate lunch together. I had asked them in class if they wanted to and they said yes. I had fun spending time with them. I will try to make plans for lunch more often."

STICK-TO-ITIVENESS

Researchers have studied what personal strengths are most helpful when people take on challenges. In 2016, Angela Duckworth wrote a book on grit, which she described as sticking with and having passion for long-term goals. She found that **grit**, more than intelligence, determined success. One example she gave is National Spelling Bee champions who study every day for hours, for months on end. You probably know other examples of grit: for example, high school swimmers who rise before dawn to practice before class and practice again after school. They love swimming and their excitement is obvious. But even on a smaller scale, you can see that stick-to-itiveness and a desire to achieve are valuable for meeting challenges.

Explore Further

Look up Duckworth's grit scale for children and get your score.

From another perspective, Carol Dweck wanted to learn about different ways people deal with failure. Her research explored mindset. She said in a **fixed mindset**, "people believe their basic qualities, like their intelligence or talent, are simply fixed traits." They believe talent, not effort, creates success. For example, a person might believe they are either smart or dumb, good at something or not. People with a **growth mindset** "believe that their most basic abilities can be developed through dedication and hard work—brains and talent are just the starting point." They apply effort, alternative strategies, practice, and learning from mistakes to succeed. By the way, we all have a combination of fixed and growth mindsets. The goal is to boost the growth part of our mindset by noticing our fixed mindset and working to overcome it. Here's an example of a fixed mindset: "I'm not good at basketball." A growth mindset might sound something like "I am still learning and practicing basketball."

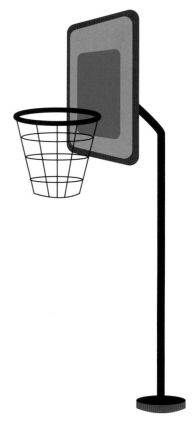

Taming Emotions

Check Out the Research

In a series of studies, Dweck and her colleagues compared the performance and attitudes of kids who were praised for being smart versus those who were praised for working hard. Both groups were similar at the outset, but praise for being smart triggered a fixed mindset. Those students tended to reject a challenging new task they were told they could learn from. They didn't want to take a chance and appear not smart. In contrast, nine out of every ten of the students who were praised for their effort wanted to try the challenging new task. Then all the students were given some new hard problems. The kids who were told they were smart now thought they were not smart after all. The kids who were praised for working hard did not see the hard task as a failure even when they couldn't solve the problems. Everyone thought the first (easier) set of problems was enjoyable, but after the hard problems, the kids praised for being smart no longer liked the task, while the kids praised for their effort thought the harder problems were fun!

Did You Know?

According to surveys conducted by the Happiness Research Institute, in 2019 the three happiest countries in the world were Finland, Denmark, and Norway. Researchers asked people how satisfied they were with their lives. Freedom, access to health care, and social connections were most important to people.

THANKSGIVING ALL YEAR LONG

Quite a few countries have some sort of Thanksgiving celebration, a time to express appreciation or **gratitude**. But research shows that thankfulness shouldn't be saved for once a year. Psychologists showed that promoting thankfulness is important to the individual and to the community; it encourages cooperation and teamwork and builds positive emotion. Jeffrey Froh and colleagues asked school kids to focus either on things that they were grateful for or things that annoyed them. They found that those in the gratitude group were significantly more satisfied and showed increased well-being. They even liked school better!

Try This

Do your own informal study of gratitude. On Day 1, don't do anything differently. Just keep count of how often you say thank you and how often others say thank you to you. Note how you feel at the end of the day. On Day 2, purposely increase the number of times you say thank you to others. Again, keep count of how often you say thank you and how often others say thank you to you. Is there any difference in how you feel at the end of the day?

Positive psychology's focus on what strengths enable individuals and communities to thrive has revealed many effective strategies for bouncing back from difficulty and managing failure. The work has helped children and adults to challenge unhelpful thoughts of self-criticism and hopelessness, to express gratitude, and to increase optimism and overall well-being.

NOW YOU KNOW!

- Positive psychology is the science of what helps people to have a good life, even when we face challenges.

- What you say to yourself affects how you feel and, in turn, what you do or how you respond to various setbacks.

- Experiments in which people did or didn't have a degree of control over their environment showed that lacking control resulted in helplessness and a low mood. Even just knowing that one had some control resulted in improved performance.

- One's mental attitude (optimistic or pessimistic) has an effect on both physical and mental health.

- Resilience is a component of overall well-being. A positive and open-minded sense of self and active use of resources each contributes to overcoming set backs. Importantly, research shows that these skills can be learned.

- Excitement about a subject and stick-to-itiveness are more important than intelligence for high achievement.

- A person's mindset can encourage or discourage success.

- Expressing gratitude helps people feel good about their lives.

Chapter 17

WHAT ABOUT WHEN IT ALL FEELS LIKE TOO MUCH?

Everyone feels worried or sad sometimes. Everyone has trouble paying attention or getting along with others sometimes. So, when do feelings or behaviors or experiences become a problem? Psychologists study this question and research ways to help. They also study the **stigma** of having a mental health disorder and the shame people may feel because others don't understand and may be critical of what they are experiencing. Generally, people are comfortable going to a pediatrician or a dentist, for example, but may feel embarrassed about consulting a psychologist. You can see right away how unfair this attitude is and how harmful it is when it prevents people from getting the help they need. Hopefully, reading this book is helping you to see the complicated ways that the mind works and how what you are born with mixes with your growing-up experiences. As you learn that mental health problems are pretty common, and that many people experience mental illness at some time in their lives, perhaps you will feel that seeing a psychologist can be a good way to take care of yourself.

WHEN WORRY AND SADNESS INTERFERE

Worry and fear are natural and even necessary. They tell us danger is near. Remember fight or flight from Chapter 12? If you are a bit worried about an exam, your worry might push you to study. If you have a big game coming up, worry might get you to do some extra practice. If you are afraid of falling off your bike, you might remember to wear your helmet. But worry and fear can also cause false alarms. You can worry or be afraid when there is no actual need, or at least not enough to match the level of your worry or fear. Many kids worry too much that they are going to mess up or get sick or be laughed at. Many kids are too afraid that something terrible will happen. When worry or fear get too strong, interfere with daily life, or last a long time, then an **anxiety disorder** has taken hold.

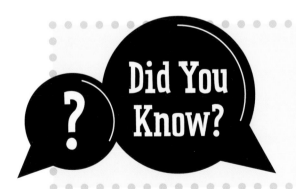

Did You Know?

Anxiety disorders are the most common mental illness in children and teens. As many as three out of ten children and teens have an anxiety disorder. The majority will never receive care from a psychologist.

As with anxiety, sadness and irritability are normal emotions. At the very least, they signal that something is bothering you that you should try to fix (or get help to fix). Research shows that being sad can improve attention to details, judgment, sticking with tasks, and your ability to make more convincing arguments. So, sadness is not by itself good or bad.

Check Out the Research

Joseph Forgas and his research team conducted observations in a newspaper shop in Australia. They observed one group of people on days when the weather was bad, and the researchers played sad music to add to a gloomy mood. The other group was observed on days when the weather was bright and sunny, and they played happy music. Both groups spent the same short amount of time in the shop. Ten small objects were placed around the cash register. The researchers asked people outside the shop as they left to recall the items. The gloomy mood group had a better memory! The researchers concluded that being in a sad mood makes people pay better attention to the little things around them.

But as with anxiety, too much sadness is a different matter. Being sad or down a lot of the time for a long time, so much so that it interferes with school or sleep or friendships or other important aspects of daily life, is known as **depression**. About three out of every hundred kids aged three to 17 have diagnosed depression.

The good news is that helpful treatments are available for both anxiety and depression. One treatment called **Cognitive Behavioral Therapy** principles teaches people to replace unhelpful thoughts with helpful, more realistic ways of thinking. Research has shown that this can lead to more positive feelings and better coping. We call well-researched treatments **evidence-based**.

Try This

Everyone has some unhelpful thoughts. Learning how to challenge them takes time and practice. Here are a few examples:

UNHELPFUL THOUGHT	CHALLENGE THOUGHT
Nobody likes me.	I did have fun playing with my neighbor yesterday and he seemed to have fun too.
I'll probably fail the test.	I will study hard and do my best.
My parents never let me do anything fun.	They want me in on a school night, but they did take my friend and me to the movies last weekend.

Now try challenging these unhelpful thoughts:

When I missed the ball, I made my team lose.	
Everybody has more cool stuff than me.	
My book report will be the worst one.	

WHEN ANGER BECOMES A PROBLEM

Anger is an emotion that we need. It tells us there is a problem that needs to be dealt with. But anger itself can easily become a problem when it leads to **aggression**, or behaviors that hurt another person, whether in words or actions. Under age four, children have tantrums, as many as nine a week. Over age four, if tantrums continue, they are likely to cause problems in school or in the home. Not being able to control angry outbursts is the most common reason children are seen by mental health professionals.

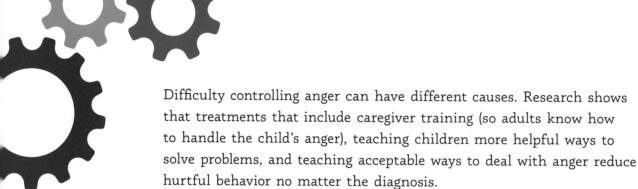

Difficulty controlling anger can have different causes. Research shows that treatments that include caregiver training (so adults know how to handle the child's anger), teaching children more helpful ways to solve problems, and teaching acceptable ways to deal with anger reduce hurtful behavior no matter the diagnosis.

Learning to control anger is an important part of growing up. Here are some steps:

- Recognize the feeling—don't push anger away. Notice the feeling and name it: Yup, I'm angry.

- Think helpful thoughts—instead of "I can't handle this" try "I'm angry because…"

- Say what you need without hurting—"I don't like when you come in my room without knocking."

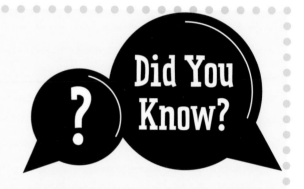

Did You Know?

Look back at Chapter 14 for some research about ways to stay calm.

TOO MUCH AND NOT ENOUGH

All living creatures must eat to stay alive and healthy. For humans, however, eating too much or too little can become a problem. In the past, an **eating disorder** was seen mostly as a problem faced by older teens and adults, but it turns out that many kids suffer with problem-eating as well. Some avoid eating or severely limit what they eat out of a fear of getting fat. They may come to believe that they are fat and see themselves as overweight when they look in the mirror even if they are, in fact, too skinny. While kids with this type of eating disorder have a strong need to be in control of their weight, others lose control of their eating and overeat. They may eat a lot of high calorie foods a lot of the time and become overweight or their overeating may come in bursts with normal eating or even undereating at times. Both eating too little and eating too much can lead to later health problems and even interfere with normal development and school performance. When a kid is trying to overcome an eating disorder, parents and caregivers are included in treatment. That treatment may include education about nutrition, a plan of positive reinforcement of healthier eating, and addressing inaccurate ways that the individual is seeing themselves.

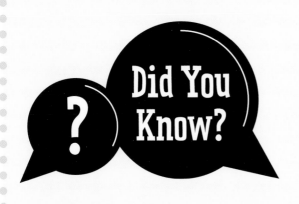

Did You Know?

Advertising of junk food has been shown to be related to obesity in children. Young children think that ads during a favorite show are part of the show. TV is TV! They're not as easily able to separate the fun, colorful ads from the fun, colorful show. They don't realize that the companies advertising junk food are trying to sell them something—they just know they want it.

WHEN REALLY BAD THINGS HAPPEN

Sometimes people, including kids, experience really bad events like a terrible accident or a fire. While many are able to bounce back after a period of being upset, others may continue to suffer difficulties that make returning to regular life hard. If someone has had a really terrible experience, they may experience nightmares, be super sensitive, or feel overwhelmed with the same feelings they had at the time of the event (especially when something triggers a memory of the event). Or, they may feel depressed and withdrawn. If these problems don't seem to be getting better in time, the person may be experiencing **Post-Traumatic Stress Disorder (PTSD).** PTSD can be treated by making sure the person is in a very safe place with people around to support them and then providing opportunities for them (usually as a part of working with a therapist) to talk about the experience they had if they wish to and to examine frightening, but unlikely, thoughts that the bad experience will happen again.

TROUBLE PAYING ATTENTION

Everyone has trouble paying attention sometimes and everyone can pay attention well sometimes. But when someone has trouble paying attention a lot, along with a tendency to act before thinking, they may have **Attention-Deficit/Hyperactivity Disorder** or ADHD. About nine out of every 100 kids have ADHD, a disorder you are born with, and symptoms show at a young age. Although many people with ADHD end up doing well, it can interfere with learning and making friends. Treatments include certain medicines, learning how to stay organized, and stress management. Sometimes other kinds of help, like tutoring, are also needed. ADHD begins in childhood and can be lifelong. There has been a lot of research on ADHD, much of which looks at what helps people do well in school and at work.

Other research has looked at what strengths people with ADHD tend to have. Holly White found that people with ADHD tend to think more creatively. For example, she asked her research participants to draw and describe a fruit that might exist on a planet very different from Earth. Participants with ADHD invented fruits less like fruits on Earth with unusual features like hammers and antennae. She wondered if a more distracted and less organized mind might lead to the ability to think in a creative and original way. Psychologists have also searched for a better understanding of the high activity level in most people with ADHD. Does a high activity level help in any way? Research shows it might help the brains of kids with ADHD stay focused.

Check Out the Research

Dustin Saver and team attached a digital video camera to the ceiling to record attention and activity level during several tasks given to children with and without ADHD. The kids were seated in chairs with wheels so there was plenty of opportunity to move around. They were given a computerized test of memory for numbers and letters. They needed to put the numbers in counting order and say the letter last. For example, if given 4 H 6 2, they would respond 2 4 6 H. As expected, kids with ADHD moved around more and were more distracted than non-ADHD kids. But, here's the interesting finding: the more the kids with ADHD moved around, the better they did on the memory task. The researchers think that movement may have pumped up the brains of the kids with ADHD.

Explore Further

In the last few years, schools have experimented with different amounts of activity before and during lessons. Check out desks with foot pedals, treadmill desks for kids, wobble chairs, and stability balls for active sitting. While research hasn't studied each of these pieces of equipment to know what's best, it does seem that movement helps with learning, at least for some kids.

A DIFFERENT PATH OF DEVELOPMENT

Some children develop differently than most of their peers due to **Autism Spectrum Disorder.** Children on the spectrum vary in how serious their differences are, ranging from never developing speech to doing fine in a regular classroom. People on the autism spectrum have a lot of trouble understanding how to have a relationship with people. They typically struggle to understand or talk about feelings. They can have difficulty with taking turns talking and listening and adjusting to change. They also sometimes get extra-focused on a few specific interests.

About 1 or 2 in a hundred kids are diagnosed with autism. The earlier that kids get help, the better, according to research. While autism cannot be cured, one treatment that has shown good research results in improving language, thinking skills, and better behavior is called **Applied Behavior Analysis** or ABA. It is based on the kinds of learning principles presented in Chapter 7. Goals are broken down into small steps and taught one-on-one using positive reinforcement. ABA works best when done in a fun and play-based setting. At one time, ABA was often overly harsh and demanding, but today it is meant to take what a child is already doing and build on that using lots of praise and other positive reinforcement.

Good job!

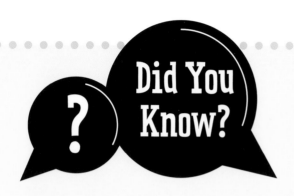

Did You Know?

Dan Aykroyd, one of the writers of the original *Ghostbusters* movie, was diagnosed with autism. He says that his deep interest in ghosts was one of his symptoms. Also, he always carries a police badge, and says he doesn't feel right without it. Aykroyd reports that his differences helped him to create comedy.

Temple Grandin is a well-known speaker and writer who talks about her experiences on the autism spectrum. She got her doctorate in animal science and became an expert on how to handle cattle in a respectful way. If you look online you will find that she has written books (including some for kids) explaining how autism helps her understand animals. There are also YouTube interviews of her.

Psychologists have made great strides in better understanding these conditions and in finding treatments that help. Seeing a psychologist to get help is part of getting and staying mentally healthy.

NOW YOU KNOW!

- Problems with feelings, behaviors, or experiences can cause distress and interfere in daily life so much that they are mental illnesses. It's best if people feel okay about getting help.

- Anxiety disorders are the most common childhood mental illness.

- It's okay to be sad or down, but too much for too long can interfere with daily life and needs treatment.

- Cognitive-Behavioral Therapy treats anxiety disorders and depression.

- A problem with anger can have many possible causes. It is the most common reason children are seen by mental health professionals.

- Both undereating and overeating can interfere with health as well as aspects of daily life. Some kids may need treatment for an eating disorder.

- Attention-Deficit/Hyperactivity Disorder is present at birth and causes symptoms at a young age. Movement may actually help ADHD kids perform better.

- Some children with certain developmental differences may have Autism Spectrum Disorder. While there is no cure at this time, evidenced-based treatments such as Applied Behavior Analysis are available.

Part 8

LIVING WITH OTHERS

Chapter 18

WHY ARE OTHER PEOPLE SO IMPORTANT?

Think of all the people in your life: your family, your classmates, your neighbors, and the many other people you see each day. Humans developed to live and have relationships with other humans. Even when you are alone, you operate as a social creature, choosing to engage in entertainment (the internet, books, movies) and even thoughts that include others. Why are other people so important to you? How do you choose who to spend time with? How does the presence of other people influence you?

Your family members are the most important people in your life, the foundation for your later relationships. Who you choose to spend time with and your expectations of others are built upon your earliest experiences with your first caregivers. As you grew, you began to interact with people outside of your family, choosing friends and expanding social experiences. There are many reasons that people become friends. Some seem obvious and logical. Think about your own friends. They probably like doing the same things you like to do. They probably live close to you or spend time in the same places as you. Their daily activities and experiences are likely to be similar to yours, too. Some reasons may be less obvious. Do you have some friends who seem very different from you? You may have become interested in them precisely because they knew about things that you didn't. And sometimes a first impression or things you heard before you met a person can also draw you to them.

FIRST IMPRESSIONS MEAN A LOT!

You may have heard people talk about making a "first impression." But are the first things you notice about someone lasting? It turns out that not only are they lasting, but they are likely to have a bigger impact on how you view that person's personality than later shared experiences! Psychologists call this the **primacy effect**.

Check Out the Research

In a famous study from the 1940s, psychologist Solomon Asch assigned research participants to one of two experiences. The first group was given a positive description of a person first, then later heard negative information about that person. They tended to see that person as having positive personality traits and saw the negative things they heard about as minor or temporary. If they first heard the negative description, that became the way they viewed that person even when they heard good things about them later.

Imagine if a new kid joined your class and was friendly and taught you and your friends a cool new magic trick! If that same kid got mad and yelled at the teacher the next week, you might think, "Poor John! He must be frustrated moving to a new school." And the teacher would probably think the same thing. But what if John yelled at the teacher the first day, even before the kids had a chance to play? The kids and even the teacher might feel less interested in seeing his sunny smile or magic trick the next week.

BIRDS OF A FEATHER BECOME FRIENDS TOGETHER!

Luckily, with time and more experiences with a person, those first impressions tend to fade gradually. While people may find different things attractive about other people, there are some general trends that draw certain people together.

You are more likely to become friends with certain types of people:

People who have similar interests and ideas. After all, you are likely to have a better time with someone who likes doing the things you like to do and sees the world the way you do.

People who are different from you in a helpful way. While we tend to like people who are like us, too much similarity can be boring. A friend who has a new idea to share or who knows how to do something you don't know how to do can add interest. And sometimes a buddy who is good at something you struggle with can make life easier. If you're quiet, it's nice to have a friend who is more comfortable speaking up.

People you see often. The more time you spend with someone, the more shared experiences you can talk about and the more likely it is that you have developed interests in the same games, books, music, and other interests. Chances are you'll also share the same friends.

People who are good (but not perfect) at doing things. We like people who do things well, but when people are too good at something, it can start to feel as if you're not good enough in comparison.

People who look nice. Although it may not seem fair, research shows that people tend to like other people who fit the expectations of attractiveness set by society. Those people rated as nice-looking are seen as friendlier and more fun than less attractive people, even when people are just looking at photographs of strangers.

People who like you. Hey, who wouldn't want to hang out with someone who appreciates them?

WHY ALL THIS FOCUS ON OTHER PEOPLE?

What if you were all alone in the world? It would be hard, if not impossible, to survive! As a kid, adults in your world provide you with a place to live, food, an education, and a way to get from here to there. Other kids help you have fun, share ideas, and keep you company. And it's not just kids that need other people. Adults do as well. Because other people are very important, they can have a strong influence on our behavior. Psychologists have long been curious about that influence, when it is helpful and when it can lead to problems.

Check Out the Research

People tend to be most comfortable when everyone around them agrees. This can lead people to agree with others even when they are agreeing about something that is wrong! Solomon Asch found some really surprising results about just how wrong people were willing to be to fit in with others.

He showed people two cards. One had just one line on it while the other had three lines, one of which was the same length as the one on the first card.

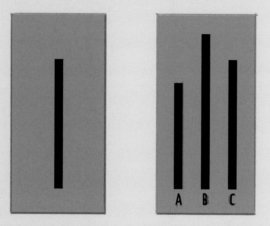

Then he asked people which of the three lines was the same as the one on the first card. BUT...the people in the experiment were put with a group of actors who were told to give the wrong answer. That was enough **peer pressure** to get one out of three people to agree with that wrong answer!

GOING ALONG TO GET ALONG

We care a lot about what others think of us and that may well explain why people would agree with others who were clearly incorrect. Because we care so much about other's opinions, we carefully work at looking and acting in ways that we think others will like. This is called **impression management** and these efforts to put our best foot forward can even be seen in the brain. What's really interesting, though, is that we seem to do this all the time. So much so that researchers can only see those changes in the brain when they ask people to *try to look bad*. Trying to look good is just the normal way of operating!

Trying to look good and get along may cause people to behave in ways they wouldn't normally. That's what underlies peer pressure, and adults are just as vulnerable to it as kids. But peer pressure can sometimes lead to changes in behavior for the better, as psychologist Robert Cialdini discovered.

Check Out the Research

Robert Cialdini did an experiment in a park to show this. The park was the Petrified Forest where ancient trees have turned to stone over many years. The park was having a problem because people would sometimes take a stone as a souvenir.

To figure out the best way to get them to stop, he put up signs in part of the park which said, "Please don't remove the petrified wood from the park, in order to preserve the natural state of the Petrified Forest." These signs just asked people to stop taking the stones. In another section signs said, "Many past visitors have removed the petrified wood from the park, changing the natural state of the Petrified Forest." These signs let visitors know that other people had broken the rules before them. Guess which sign worked best? The experiment showed that people who knew that others had broken the rules stole three times as many stones as people who were just asked not to take them.

Many past visitors have removed the petrified wood from the park, changing the natural state of the Petrified Forest.

WHO SAYS SO?

While we all tend to want to go along with others, the likelihood that we will is also influenced by aspects of the group itself. A somewhat larger group may have a stronger effect than just one other person. You are more likely to go along with the group if they all agree. It's hard to be the only one with a different opinion. And while peer pressure can be intense, you are more likely to do what an **authority figure** tells you to do than if directions come from a peer, because authority figures by definition have power and influence.

Try This

Design a sign to encourage people to clean up their dog's poop. What would you want it to say? Who might you want the sign to be written by—a kid, an adult, the mayor of the town?

I WILL IF THEY DO BUT I WON'T IF THEY DON'T!

It seems obvious that one of the advantages of being social animals is that groups of humans can accomplish more than individuals could do on their own. Working in groups, humans have been able to build tall buildings, dig tunnels large enough for cars to drive through, and design ships that fly into outer space! Clearly teamwork offers incredible advantages.

But it turns out that teamwork is not always the best way to get everyone to work hard. It depends on workers' awareness of how hard others are working! If everyone

can easily see each individual person's effort, each member of the team tends to work harder. But if the work requires a group of people to contribute effort to the same task and you can't tell how hard each person is working (like pulling a rope in a tug of war), each person works a little less hard than they would otherwise.

THE YEAR KIDS PUT A ROCK ON THEIR HOLIDAY WISH LIST

One way to influence people is to tell them what everyone else is doing. Knowing how others act can influence us in positive or negative ways. In the mid-1970s, a young man was listening to his friends talk about how much work it took to care for their pets. He decided the world's easiest pet would be a rock. So, he developed the "Pet Rock": a smooth stone packaged in a cardboard box which had "air holes" and came with a care manual. Pet Rocks became a very popular holiday gift. Each sold for about $4 and their creator became a millionaire. Why would so many people spend money to buy something they could easily make themselves? Why would they want such a thing in the first place? Having read this far, I'm sure you know the answer: it seemed like everyone else was doing it! This kind of instant popularity of something is referred to as a fad or a craze (and sometimes they do seem a bit "crazy"). Pet Rocks are certainly not the first nor the last.

Try This

Make a list of all the fads you can think of. Consider toys, books, shows, music, activities, and on and on! How long is your list? Ten things, twenty, thirty, more? Ask your parents and grandparents what fads were around when they were young and add those to your list.

WHAT WOULD YOU DO IN AN EMERGENCY? IT MIGHT DEPEND UPON WHO ELSE IS THERE!

The presence and behavior of other people changes the way people think and act. You might expect that, in an emergency, people would seek help right away. But it turns out that that might not be true if they're around other people, especially if the other people are acting as if it's no big deal! If others are with you, you may not feel as responsible to get help. And, if they are not acting as if there is an emergency, you may be less likely to see the problem as urgent. This failure to act is called the **bystander effect** and it has sometimes led to people not calling 911 in a serious emergency.

Check Out the Research

Bibb Latane and John Darley did many experiments on the bystander effect. In one they found that if three people were in a room that starts to fill with smoke, they are much less likely to jump up and run for help than if they are alone. When participants were alone, most (about three of every four) went to get the experimenter. But if there were two actors who ignored the smoke, very few (one of every ten) reported it.

Humans have evolved as social animals. So, it makes sense that we spend much of our lives making and keeping connections to others and rely on what other people do to understand what is happening around us. Sometimes others can influence our judgements and behavior in surprising ways.

NOW YOU KNOW!

○ Your first impression of someone has a big impact on how you view them and their later behavior.

○ People tend to like others who are similar to them and who seem to like them.

○ Humans are agreeable creatures. We are likely to agree with the opinions of others around us, even if they are incorrect!

○ Peer pressure has a strong impact on everyone, even adults. While this is sometimes a bad thing, knowing that other people are doing something good can convince us to do it as well.

○ People are less likely to take responsibility to act in an emergency if others around them aren't taking action to help.

Chapter 19

HOW CAN YOU UNDERSTAND OTHER PEOPLE'S EXPERIENCES?

Have you ever had the experience of walking into a friend's house and getting a sense that the rules are somewhat different than what you're used to? Maybe you usually take your shoes off at the door and your friend doesn't. Or, maybe people in your friend's family tend to come into a room to talk to someone when you're used to yelling from room to room. If you've ever visited a house of worship of a religion different than your own, you are even more likely to immediately feel that there are unwritten rules that regular attendees know. They might include types of clothing, head coverings, silence or talking, a variety of body postures, and so on.

Hey, Mom, can we have a snack?

Groups have unwritten rules for behavior called **social norms**. They help the group feel connected and also may identify who belongs to that group. Groups share other types of knowledge as well. Words may mean one thing to members of one group and something else to those from another. Different groups may share different speech patterns and different languages, and nonverbal cues may have different meanings. Behavior that is unacceptable in one group may be typical in another. For a newcomer, there's an awful lot to pay attention to, but for members of the group these behaviors are expected and automatic.

WHY FORM GROUPS IN THE FIRST PLACE?

Knowing social norms simplifies life. It helps you predict and understand the behavior of others. Shared experiences and knowledge make communications go more smoothly with fewer misunderstandings. At a very basic level, identifying as belonging to one group reduces the amount of information a person needs to decide whether someone is a threat or a support. For ancient humans this was important to their very survival. Being with others in your group also provides information about what different behaviors mean and which types of behavior will be accepted by other members and which will lead you to be criticized or rejected.

This strategy can work very well in some situations. It's helpful when sports teams wear different color uniforms so you can tell which group they belong to. Visual cues, in particular, can be processed quickly and easily. But the tendency to put people into groups based on a small bit of information can be problematic, especially because it often leads to an assumption that all the individuals in that group are the same in other ways.

Try This

These are the 'jocks'

Of course, calling a group of people "jocks" is a stereotype. What kinds of assumptions might someone make about someone called a "jock"? Which things would be surprising to learn about them?

- They run fast
- They practice a musical instrument every day
- They laugh at dirty jokes
- They like pizza
- They prefer being in a group rather than being alone
- They prefer being alone to being in a group
- They are loud
- They love reading
- They're shy
- They work well with other people
- They like to bake

While some of the things on this list (those directly related to athletics) make sense, others could just as likely be true (or not true) of someone that other people categorize as "jocks."

THE COST OF SOCIAL EFFICIENCY

While categorizing groups of people helps us function more efficiently in the social world, this strategy comes at a price. By relying on easily available cues to decide who belongs in which group, we also overlook differences between group members. That means we are more likely to think that the people in the group are more similar than they really are and to assign the same characteristics to all members of that group. This is called stereotyping.

You've probably heard the word "stereotype" before! A stereotype is a kind of shortcut, but one that is full of errors. When we simplify the world by putting people into categories, we oversimplify what they are like and inaccurately limit our ideas of how members of those categories act. Stereotyping can be positive ("tall people are good at basketball") or negative ("short people aren't good at basketball").

Try This

Write down two of your physical characteristics and some assumptions someone might make about you that are wrong.

Physical Characteristic

Looks Young		
Doesn't read except for school Doesn't know anything about psychology		

Assumptions

When stereotyped views are negative, they often result in **prejudice.** You can think of the word "prejudice" as being a judgement about someone before (**"pre"**) knowing them. These are generally negative views of people based on their appearance or the group they belong to.

How Can You Understand Other People's Experiences?

WHERE DOES PREJUDICE COME FROM?

Prejudice can develop through hearing what others say about the group, observing how they treat them, or seeing some members of that group displaying negative behaviors (or not displaying positive ones). For example, prejudices about how girls should act could develop from hearing things like "girls cry easily, they are sensitive." Or by seeing others regularly ask girls to help cook and boys to help with yard work. Or if there are very few books or shows where girls are depicted as interested in science.

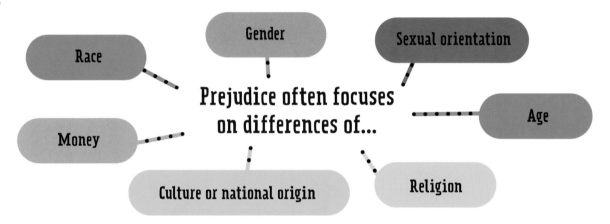

Prejudice often focuses on differences of...

Race · Gender · Sexual orientation · Age · Religion · Culture or national origin · Money

I SEE THE PROOF ALL AROUND ME!

Stereotypes and prejudice can become reinforced through **confirmation bias**: the tendency to see and believe things that support what we already think and ignore signs that our prior assumptions are incorrect.

See, there is proof that aliens exist.

That looks like the blimp that flies over football games.

Confirmation bias can strengthen inaccurate negative views of others. In 2001, after the United States was attacked by terrorists on 9/11, it was learned that the attacks were carried out by terrorists who practiced an extremist version of Islam. People who were afraid of another attack, and who had limited experience with Islam, began to be very fearful of all Muslim people (people who practice Islam). Islamic mosques were unfairly seen by some as meeting grounds for terrorists rather than the religious centers that they are. Innocent Muslim people were treated with suspicion and anger.

MAKING JUDGEMENTS IN A SNAP

The process of categorizing people into groups can occur so fast that we don't even realize it's happening! These snap judgements, which include negative assumptions, are called **implicit bias**. Implicit bias can lead to unfair treatment of others, like turning someone down for a job because they are older, being more critical of women candidates for political office than men, and over-aggressively policing people of color. Even people who don't think they discriminate sometimes do because their negative associations occur so quickly and without awareness. It's really hard to fix implicit biases because people don't realize they have them and don't want to think that they do. But taking a hard look at our assumptions about other people, and working to adjust them, is a step toward making the world a better place.

IF EVERYONE THINKS I AM, MAYBE I AM!

Stereotypes can even influence how people see themselves. This can happen because of how they are treated by others and because of what they hear others say about them. They may then act in ways that fit the stereotype. Such **self-fulfilling prophecies** then confirm others' beliefs about members of that group. Although some stereotypes may contain some amount of truth about differences between groups, they are inaccurately applied to all members of the group. For example, in general, boys tend to be less interested in babies than girls are. But that doesn't mean that all girls like playing with babies or that many boys don't enjoy them. But if people around them think boys aren't into babies, they may not ask a boy if he'd like to hold the baby. The boy may then feel awkward asking to play with the baby and go off to play with his toy train. Observers may see this as proof that "babies aren't for boys."

Try This

Do you think of some of these things as "boy things" and others as "girl things"?

- Wearing dresses
- Playing basketball
- Arts and crafts
- Using a hand drill
- Using an electric mixer
- Knitting
- Playing with electric trains

- Forgetting to take off cleats before walking in the house
- Burping loudly
- Spending a lot of time fixing hair
- Reading
- Solving math puzzles

- Cleaning
- Being a dancer
- Being a firefighter

Do you think any of your answers have changed since learning about stereotyping?

WHEN THE CATEGORY IS RACE

Sometimes stereotypes and prejudice are based on long-standing tensions between groups because of historical events. This can lead to negative views of people from a different country, ethnic group, or skin color. Prejudice against Black people in the United States grew out of slavery. During slavery, Black people kidnapped from Africa were labeled as inferior beings as a justification for enslaving them. Fears that they may try to fight back led to many White Americans seeing enslaved Black people as potentially threatening. This association between people with dark skin and these incorrect views of slaves was extended to Black people who were not slaves (free Black people and Africans who came to this country after slavery ended), and many of the stereotypes developed during slavery and shortly after persist today. We know that hair color and texture, skin color, and other physical traits have nothing to do with whether a person is rich or poor, violent or peaceful, a good student or a bad one. But what we hear from others or see in the media can spread these impressions.

Did You Know?

Babies as young as 6 months old tend to gaze longer at adults of the same race, suggesting that they have learned to identify which racial group is "theirs."

Sometimes the way these attitudes are communicated to others and even to subsequent generations can be hard to recognize. For example, we might not be surprised if a White person raised in a family that regularly talks badly about Black people develops a negative view of them. But something as simple as the *absence* of positive views of a group can also reinforce stereotypes—like when books, movies, and television have far fewer heroes and main characters of color than White ones. It makes our brains associate *hero* with *White* without ever saying it.

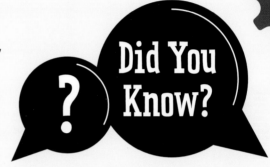

Did You Know?

We tend to talk about race as if it's an inborn quality, but labeling someone as Black, White, or Latinx is based on how they look or the cultural group they belong to, not genetic differences. Many Black people in the United States have White ancestors. People who identify as Latinx may originally come from Spanish-speaking countries, but also from places where Portuguese is spoken. They may have some ancestors who were European colonizers, Indigenous Peoples of South America, and/or Africans.

Check Out the Research

Black school children, and especially Black boys, tend to be referred for discipline more often than White peers.

Walter Gilliam and his research team had preschool teachers watch videos of children doing a variety of activities. They asked the teachers to register on a keypad each time they saw a child do something that might potentially become a behavior problem. At the same time, he used a machine that tracked where the teachers' eyes were focused. They found that preschool teachers who were on the lookout for bad behavior looked at the Black children more than the White children and, in particular, spent more time looking at Black boys. This suggested that the teachers had an implicit bias that bad behavior would more often be exhibited by those students.

HOW CAN WE FIGHT NEGATIVE STEREOTYPES, BIAS, AND PREJUDICE?

Stereotypes, prejudice, and implicit biases are unfair and often destructive. Many researchers have been interested in whether these attitudes can change with experience. Psychologist Thomas Pettigrew looked at over 500 studies completed over sixty years. He concluded from the findings that simply having contact with members of another group wasn't enough to challenge biases. But when people had friendships with members of a different race or culture, they were far less prejudiced and hostile towards the other group. So, building relationships between people may be key.

Check Out the Research

Sarah Gaither and Samuel Sommers looked at what impact living with a roommate of a different race might have. Their research found that after four months the White students who were assigned non-White roommates developed more diverse friendships and valued diversity more than did those who roomed with other White students. After six months they were more relaxed when faced with interracial experiences than were the students who roomed with White students.

Judging others in unfair and prejudicial ways is an unfortunate by-product of our need to reduce information about our social world. This process has resulted in the development of inaccurate negative views of others and to centuries of mistreatment of some groups of people. One way to work toward overcoming prejudice and negative bias is to have people interact in ways that allow them to see individuals more accurately and completely.

NOW YOU KNOW!

○ The social norms of a group help members interact efficiently with one another.

○ In our efforts to simplify our social relationships, we tend to assign people who do not belong to our group to another group and then make assumptions about those groups (stereotyping).

○ We're more likely to believe information that agrees with the ideas we already have (about people, or, really, anything).

○ Our automatic judgements about others based on their appearance and group membership sometimes happen so rapidly that we're not even aware of them.

○ Being assigned to a group, and knowing the stereotypes of members of that group, can actually make it more likely that members will start to fit those stereotypes.

○ Negative stereotypes and prejudices can be lessened by developing personal relationships between members of different groups.

Chapter 20

IS CONFLICT PART OF BEING HUMAN?

Have you ever gotten into an argument with your sibling? Has anyone ever bullied you, or have you ever bullied someone (or picked on someone else)? Do you hear loud disagreements between adults on the radio and TV? Do you sometimes wish people would just get along? Humans seem to have had conflicts with other humans for as long as we've been around. What does psychological research tell us about why people hurt one another (both physically and emotionally), why they sometimes offer support to another person under attack, and what can reduce conflicts between people?

WHEN GROUPS CLASH

When a person belongs to a group, it changes their behavior and thinking. Members of a group tend to have greater empathy for those within the group and less empathy for outsiders. When the groups are especially different, the inability to put oneself in the place of outsiders makes it easier to treat them unfairly or even aggressively. The social pressure of the group pushes members to greater agreement with one another, reluctance to question the social norms of the group, and more extreme views. This is called **group think**. Over time, this process can lead to distorted views of outsiders, hostile feelings between groups, and even to aggression.

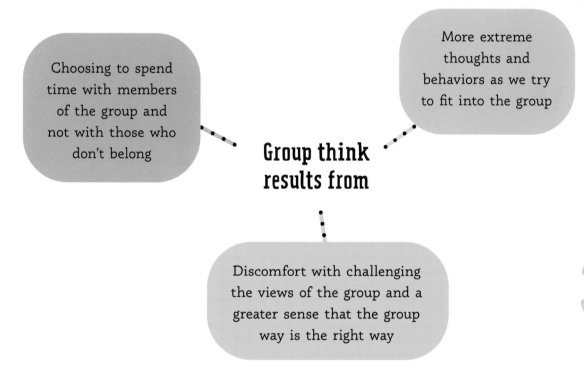

Choosing to spend time with members of the group and not with those who don't belong

More extreme thoughts and behaviors as we try to fit into the group

Group think results from

Discomfort with challenging the views of the group and a greater sense that the group way is the right way

REDUCING TENSION BETWEEN GROUPS

Elliot Aronson explored whether working together could help to build better relationships between racial groups. In 1971 in Texas, schools were required to desegregate (at that time, Texas schools still had primarily White students or students of color). Previously separated racial and cultural groups began to clash with one another. To try to reduce conflict between the groups, Aronson developed what he called the "jigsaw classroom": small, racially mixed groups of students were forced to work cooperatively.

Each student was responsible for researching one aspect of material to be learned and then teaching their group about it. Then, each student was tested on all the material. This meant that everyone on the team was dependent upon all the others to do well. The results were hopeful. Weaker students were helped by stronger students, who needed them to gather important information. Compared to more traditional classrooms, students learned more and felt better about themselves as learners. But, one of the best outcomes was that negative views of other racial groups were reduced.

WHEN INDIVIDUAL PEOPLE HURT OTHERS

Aggression evolved out of early humans' needs to protect themselves from attack and to help them stand their ground in the competition for food, territory, and mates. To some degree, then, aggression is built into human nature. While you are likely to think of aggression in terms of causing physical harm, **social aggression** (such as excluding others) and **verbal aggression** (such as name calling) can be painful as well. **Sexual harassment,** unwelcome and inappropriate sexual remarks or physical advances, is also a form of aggression. It is particularly unnerving and must be reported to a trusted adult.

While most people no longer have to rely on aggression to stay safe or to obtain what they need, aggressive impulses can still be triggered. People are more likely to act aggressively if they are experiencing negative emotions and especially if they are frustrated. Aggression can also result from watching the aggression of others, as in Albert Bandura's social learning experiments that you read about in Chapter 7. With a lot of exposure to violence, people can become used to it and less likely to try to stop their own violent reactions.

Check Out the Research

A 2002 study by Craig Bushman and Brad Anderson had volunteers play either a violent or a nonviolent videogame for 20 minutes. They then read them stories about people having conflicts and asked what thoughts, actions, and feelings would happen next. Participants who had played the violent games were more likely to think that the story characters would feel more anger and act more aggressively than the participants who had played nonviolent games did. The aggression from the game spilled over into the participants' next activity.

THE AGGRESSION OF BULLIES

Bullying is different than some other forms of aggression in that it is always intended to hurt another and involves one person or group (the bully) who has power over another (the victim). Bullying is so common that, in a national survey, 70 percent of middle and high school students indicated having experienced some form of bullying. But for some kids, being the victim of bullying can be ongoing and interfere with their lives. Bullying has been found to impact students' performance in school and can lead to self-blame ("I deserve to be picked on") and even depression.

Although it is sometimes said that bullies are insecure, lonely kids who are struggling to be accepted, research doesn't seem to back that up. In fact, psychologists who have studied bullying have found that bullies tend to have lots of friends and to be seen by others as "cool." They don't tend to be insecure and, in fact, sometimes see themselves in a very positive way. Victims of bullying, on the other hand, tend to be more insecure, anxious, and lonely than others of their age.

Bullying in younger children can often involve a larger, stronger child physically attacking a peer. As kids move into middle and high school, social aggression is more common and often involves excluding a victim or spreading rumors about them. **Cyberbullying**, online harassment, is often directed at victims who are also being targeted in other ways but has added complications. Since cyberbullying involves fast communication that is easily spread over social media, a large community is quickly reached. Online bullying makes it easy for the bully to hide their identity and difficult for adults to monitor or offer help.

While discussions of bullying often focus on the bullies and victims, others are also typically involved directly and indirectly with these conflicts. It's common for peers to be witnesses or bystanders. Some may assist the bully by joining in or encouraging them. Others may simply stand by, giving passive support to the bully. Only in about one out of four cases do others try to help the victim. In part, this may be out of fear of being the bully's next victim.

Psychologists agree that effective programs to stop bullying need to focus on individual kids, their families, and the culture of the school. And, given the significant impact of bullying on victims, it is important that kids who have been bullied be supported and helped to recover.

FOLLOWING THE LEADER

Some people have a great deal of influence over the behavior of others. Psychologists call this **social power**. One source of this power is a position of authority over the other: Parents and teachers have social power over kids, bosses have social power over employees.

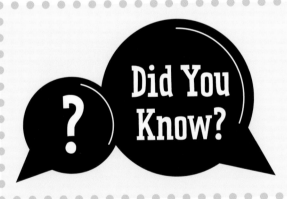

Psychologist Stanley Milgram devised an experiment to explore how willing people would be to obey the directions of an authority figure. His findings were disturbing! Research participants were told they were going to be in a study on learning. They were told they would serve as "teachers" and other participants, who would be in another room, would be assigned to be "learners." What the "teachers" didn't know was that the "learners" actually left. They were replaced by pre-taped audio recordings used to communicate with "teachers."

When the recordings indicated that the learners had made a mistake on a task that asked them to memorize pairs of words, the researcher told the "teachers" to give them a shock. As time went on, the shocks they were asked to give were labeled as stronger and stronger and the recording indicated that the learners were in pain, wanted to stop the experiment, were afraid they'd have a heart attack, and finally, stopped answering. Researchers (the authority figures) insisted the experiment continue. In this experiment, well over half of participants were willing to give shocks that they thought might be deadly to strangers simply because an authority figure told them to do so.

Stop! Let me out! This really hurts!

Milgram's study has been repeated many times in different places with the same (or worse) findings. Milgram, however, believed that the social situation, not the character of the people, accounted for the willingness to hurt others at the direction of an authority. He followed up with a series of studies to see what changes in the situation might make people less likely to obey.

Having the "learner" visible to the "teacher"

Having the authority figure out of the room and communicating by phone

Changes to Milgram's study that reduced obedience to authority

Requiring the "teacher" to hold the shocking device on the "learner's" hand

Having another "teacher" refuse to proceed with shocking someone

The story of the Emperor's New Clothes is a good example of how one person, even a kid, can change how other people react to something that just doesn't seem right. In that story, all the kingdom praised how the king looked in the wonderful new clothes a clever but dishonest tailor had convinced them he had made. Things changed when a small child said what should have been obvious to all—the king had no clothes on at all! Suddenly everyone could "see" what had been in front of their eyes all along.

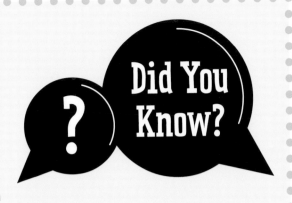

It can be hard to say you think something is wrong when others seem to be going along with it. But doing so can also help others to stand up for what's right.

HELPING IS HUMAN TOO

Of course, people do often stick up for someone being bullied and help others who are in need. Under what circumstances will people help a stranger in trouble? Psychologists have studied what circumstances make it more or less likely that people will help a stranger in trouble.

One important variable is whether other people are there and how they are reacting. The more people nearby who are witnessing a person in need but doing nothing to help, the more likely it is that others will also fail to help. A second significant source of influence on helping behavior is **ambiguity**. If it's unclear whether something is a real emergency, you are less likely to offer help. These influences may, in fact, be tied to each other. When a situation is unclear (ambiguous) you may look at the behavior of those nearby to help you make sense of how you should respond.

Check Out the Research

Psychologists Russell Clark and Larry Word arranged for participants to see a workman carrying a ladder and some venetian blinds past them as they waited to participate in an experiment. When the workman was out of sight, the participants heard a loud crash. Participants were more likely to check out whether he was okay if there were few other people around. They were also more likely to help if they heard the workman yell that he was hurt (which made the emergency less ambiguous).

It's reassuring to know that, even though having a lot of people around in an emergency makes it less likely that each person will help, research shows that most of the time *someone* will step in to help! And this is true even if the situation suggests that they may be at some risk by doing so. Researcher Richard Philpot and associates looked at videos from street cameras that had caught people getting into fights. They found that over 90 percent of the time other people stepped in to help.

While conflict between groups of people and between individuals appears to be part of the human experience, it seems that a need to cooperate with one another to get things accomplished reduces tensions and increases empathy. Research also suggests that aggressive behaviors like bullying and even fighting can be reduced when bystanders speak up for victims and challenge unkind behaviors.

NOW YOU KNOW!

○ People tend to have more empathy for people who belong to the same groups that they do. They may also tend to share the same views as other group members and find it hard to challenge the ideas that are popular with their group.

○ Tasks that require cooperation of multiple individuals to obtain a goal can help to reduce hostility between people who initially belonged to different groups in conflict with one another.

○ While many people think that bullies act the way they do because they feel insecure, this doesn't seem to be the case. In fact, bullies more often act from a position of social strength and pick on others they see as vulnerable.

○ People are less likely to follow the demands of a leader to hurt others if they can see how those others are reacting.

○ A person is less likely to help another person in need if there are other people around who are not taking action. But it is still more likely than not that *someone* will step up to help a person in distress.

Part 9

PLANNING FOR A BETTER WORLD

Chapter 21

CAN PSYCHOLOGY HELP SAVE PLANET EARTH?

Psychologists interested in environmental questions study how our surroundings affect our well-being and behavior and how we can encourage behaviors that help to preserve the natural world. What have psychologists learned about ways to effectively encourage people to take care of the **environment**? What kinds of efforts encourage recycling and reduction of waste? How can people be influenced to limit the energy use that contributes to **climate change?**

STRESSED EARTH, STRESSED US!

Problems with **pollution** of water and air threaten human health. Lead pollution (in water or peeling paint chips) has a negative effect on learning and behavior when young children are exposed. Traditional methods of generating energy result in releasing carbon into the atmosphere, and this has contributed to changes in the climate and weather patterns around the world. Intense weather events and loss of crops due to flooding and drought are extremely stressful to those impacted. Overfishing, destruction of forests, and other overuse of resources threaten people's livelihoods and the balance of the **ecosystem**. Psychologists study the impact of all these problems on human beings. Many individuals and societal groups will need to work together to solve them.

The psychological effects of extreme weather events can actually get worse over time. Of people who lived through Hurricane Katrina, the rate of Post-Traumatic Stress Disorder (PTSD) was about 15 out of 100 a few months after the storm. It rose to 21 out of 100 by one year after. The emotional trauma of living through a devastating hurricane can impact children for the rest of their lives. They may be more vulnerable to alcohol and drug addictions, to later depression, and to a variety of health problems associated with stress.

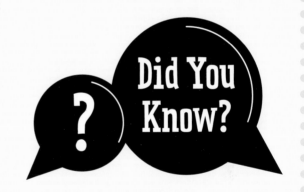

WE'RE ALL IN THIS TOGETHER!

Even those not directly impacted by natural disasters can experience anxiety and worry when they learn about these events from the news or hear predictions about what may happen to planet earth in the future. Not only is this scary, but it can leave people feeling powerless.

Global warming is increasing at an alarming rate!

Can Psychology Help Save Planet Earth?

One way to cope with feelings of helplessness in the face of such big challenges is to find ways to work to support a healthy environment. This can mean making personal choices to avoid overusing resources or adding to pollution and trying to influence other people to increase **pro-environmental behaviors**.

MAKING POSITIVE CHANGES CAN BE SMALL AND SIMPLE

People are most likely to take pro-environmental action in their immediate surroundings and when their actions have immediate results. A neighborhood cleanup of a park may only take a day's worth of effort by neighbors but makes spending time there more pleasant for all.

Research has shown that sometimes small and manageable efforts to prompt people to take care of these close-up environments can change behavior. It's probably no surprise that people are more likely to participate in caring for the environment if it is easy and inexpensive for them to do so. What is somewhat less obvious is that they are also more likely to "do the right thing" if their immediate surroundings provide cues to do so.

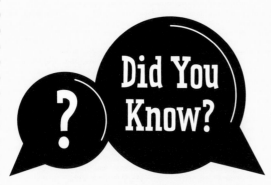

Did You Know?

People are more likely to throw away trash in a garbage can that's painted decoratively than one that's plain. Perhaps the cheerful-looking cans catch people's attention and remind them not to litter.

Check Out the Research

When people put trash into recycling bins, it makes it much more difficult and costly to process the glass, plastic, and paper into reusable material. And if recyclable items are put into the trash, they are not reused at all. Researchers Sean Duffy and Michelle Verges explored whether the design of the tops of the bins might help people to separate trash from recyclables. They studied what happened when three open bins labeled "trash," "paper," and "aluminum/glass/plastic" were used compared to the bins with the same labels that also had covers containing openings that best fit the items to be put in them.

With the specialized tops, about one third more was recycled and putting the wrong things in recycling bins decreased almost completely! That's a big difference!

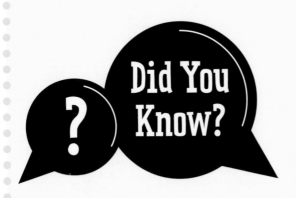

Did You Know?

Some small towns in Maine banded together and hired summer interns to give residents feedback on how well they recycled. Interns peeked into residential recycling bins to see if the contents included items like plastic bags or paper towels, which can interfere with machines that process the recycling. They then put tags on the recycling containers. People got a green tag if they recycled appropriately, a yellow tag if they had a few nonrecyclable items in their bin, and a red tag if they made a lot of mistakes. Yellow and red tags also told people what errors they had made. This short program lead to many more people participating in recycling. The amount of "contamination" of recycling with things that didn't belong there was also reduced.

MESS LEADS TO MORE MESS

You have learned from previous chapters that behavior is often influenced by observations of what other people do. When it appears that rules for keeping things neat and orderly have been broken, it's more likely that they will be broken again. Psychologists have found that this can lead to more and more litter or lack of care for the environment. If people see bicycles parked where they are not allowed, they are more likely to add their own. If shopping carts are already left in the way of cars in a parking area, people are more likely to add theirs to the mess.

Check Out the Research

In the Netherlands, researcher Kees Keizer and his team conducted a series of experiments to see how graffiti and litter might influence unrelated problem behaviors. Maybe the most surprising was one where they left an envelope, which clearly contained money, sticking part of the way out of a mailbox. They found that people were less likely to steal it if the mailbox and the area around it was tidy. If the mailbox had graffiti on it or litter around it, it was twice as likely that the money would be stolen.

People are also more likely to participate in pro-environmental efforts if they feel like they're not alone in wanting to help. Learning what others in your school, neighborhood, or sports team do can make the difference between engaging in environmentally-responsible behavior or not. Signing a group pledge to make a change in behavior can result in real change, especially if it involves doing so in a public way, because it shows that lots of people are doing it. Fears about climate change are common among kids these days. Taking action toward positive change, especially by joining with others in that effort, is a productive and effective way to cope with those scary emotions.

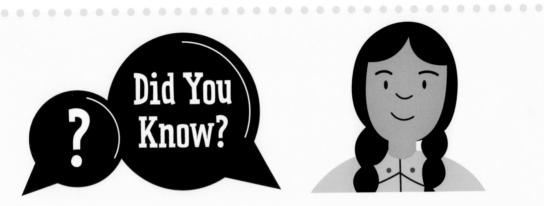

Did You Know?

Sometimes anxiety about a problem can lead people to take action. Swedish teenager, Greta Thunberg, became so upset about climate change that, at age 15, she staged a protest demanding that leaders work harder to protect against climate change. Her speeches were reported in the news and inspired teens around the world to stage school walk-outs to voice their concerns. Greta was invited to speak at the United Nations and was nominated for a Nobel Peace Prize.

BELIEVING THAT WHAT YOU DO MATTERS, MATTERS!

Simply warning people about the horrible dangers of climate change does not lead them to take steps to help the planet, and there is evidence that these scare tactics can backfire! When people are told frightening information, they may react by feeling overwhelmed and helpless and simply shut down. On the other hand, when given messages about how their behavior can help stop climate change, people are likely to make those changes. This belief that your behavior can make a difference is called **response efficacy**.

Check Out the Research

Psychologist Erika Salomon and colleagues gave different messages about climate-related response efficacy to two groups of people. The first group was told that their actions made a big difference in the fight against climate change. The other group was told that their actions would make no difference. A third group (the control group) was given no message. In the next week the participants were asked whether they had changed climate-related habits (driving less, hanging clothes to dry rather than using a dryer, using less water, or turning the heat down). People who received the message that their behaviors could lead to real change were more likely to report that they made positive changes than those in either of the other groups. And those who were told that their behavior wouldn't make a difference actually reported more energy usage than before!

It can be difficult to know what changes matter most and hard to follow through if you aren't sure they'll make a difference. The impact of behaviors is not always obvious. For example, research shows that people tend to underestimate the energy required by large household machines. In a study by Shahzeen Attari, people tended to relatively accurately judge the energy used by their computers but dramatically underestimate how much energy is needed to run their air conditioning. There is also a tendency to think that reducing how much you use something (like turning off the lights) saves more energy than using highly efficient items (like energy efficient light bulbs), which often isn't true!

Planning for a Better World

WHO'S IN THIS WITH ME?

It may seem that the best way to convince someone to conserve energy would be to explain to them why it makes sense for the environment or for themselves, but it turns out that's not true. How likely someone is to act in environmentally responsible ways is more likely to be affected by what other people are doing. Psychologist Robert Cialdini who you may remember from Chapter 1, conducted a lot of research on this kind of social influence. He found that knowing what other people do can have both positive and negative effects. For example, a message that most people don't litter could inspire people who do tend to litter to stop. On the other hand, a message that says you should stop littering because it's a big problem because so many people do it can backfire. People tend to do what others around them are doing, since they see that as the social norm.

Check Out the Research

Jessica Nolan and her team explored what kind of information was most effective in getting people to reduce energy use in their homes. They hung one of four kinds of signs on the doorknobs of four groups of households every week for a month. Then they looked at how much electric energy was used by each household. Households either got a sign suggesting that:

- they should save energy for the sake of the environment

- they should save energy for the sake of future generations

- they would save money by conserving energy

- that most of their neighbors were working to save energy every day

Only the last message reduced people's energy usage! And this was despite the fact that people thought the other reasons were important.

Try This

In a journal, on a piece of paper, or on your phone or computer, make a note of three ways that you can influence others to join you in being more energy efficient. Be as specific as you can.

- *Ask my parents to replace our incandescent light bulbs with LEDs.*

- *Tell friends I am no longer using disposable containers like plastic sandwich bags and bring lunch to school in reusable containers. Ask them if they'll join me.*

- *Research how much energy can be saved by turning down the temperature in my house in cold weather and share that information with other people.*

Now, choose one of the items from your list and follow through with it. Did your behavior change? Did anyone else's? Did you let them know you noticed?

An orderly environment contributes to physical and mental health and a safe social setting. If a person thinks caring for the environment is important to their neighbors and friends, the chances are greater that they will behave in environmentally responsible ways.

Planning for a Better World

NOW YOU KNOW!

○ Pollution can result not only in physical health problems, but can also interfere with brain development and lead to learning and behavior problems.

○ Intense weather events, like hurricanes and floods, can be highly traumatic to the people affected and result in emotional problems that can last for years.

○ Litter, graffiti, and other evidence that others have broken rules leads to additional rule-breaking behaviors.

○ Even without directly experiencing the impact of climate change, worry about it can lead to anxiety.

○ People are more likely to act in environmentally responsible ways that are manageable and local, and when they are told that their efforts have a positive impact.

○ Learning that others in one's social group or living area are contributing to caring for the environment increases environmentally responsible behavior.

Can Psychology Help Save Planet Earth?

GLOSSARY

A

Achievement motives: motives to develop abilities and succeed.

Affiliation motives: drives to have relationships and be with others.

Aggression: behaviors intended to hurt another person with words or actions.

Amygdala: a part of the brain located in the limbic system that is involved in fear, anger, and social interaction.

Anxiety Disorder: when worry or fear gets too strong and interferes with daily life.

Apophenia: the tendency to see patterns or meaning between unrelated things.

Applied Behavior Analysis: an evidence-based treatment that helps with language, communication, and other areas of developmental differences in children on the autism spectrum.

Applied psychology: the use of findings of psychological research to solve problems and help people.

Approach goals: goals based on gaining positive outcomes, such as success at a task.

Artificial intelligence: computer systems that perform like humans.

Attachment: a deep emotional bond between child and caregiver. In research, children were classified as securely attached (greeting their mother on her return), avoidant (ignoring their mother), or resistant (crying excessively when their mother left).

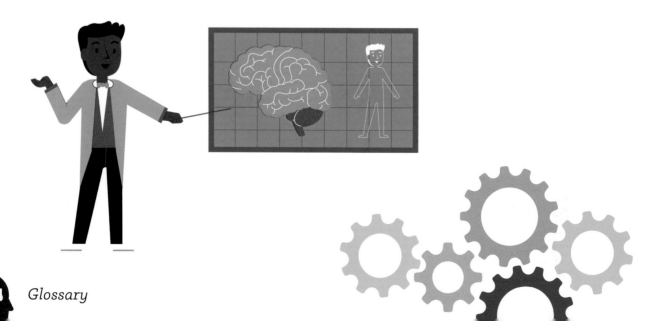

Attention-Deficit/Hyperactivity Disorder: a disorder that affects paying attention and acting without thinking.

Authority figure: a person who is in charge and has power over others. For kids this would include parents and teachers. For an adult it would include their boss.

Autism Spectrum Disorder: a disorder someone is born with that cauaes difficulties in developing relationships and understanding feelings, problems taking turns talking and listening to others, trouble adjusting to change, and getting stuck on a very few interests.

Automatic processes: thoughts and actions that are accomplished without a lot of effort and attention.

Autonomic mimicry: the automatic production of a facial expression of another person. Autonomic mimicry can occur without either person being aware of it.

Availability heuristic: a mental short cut that relies on immediate examples that come to mind.

Avoidance goals: goals based on preventing negative outcomes, such as not performing well at something.

Barnum effect: the tendency to believe vague predictions or general personality descriptions.

Behavior: how a person (or animal) acts. Behaviors are actions that other people can see..

Biological motives: drives for things necessary for biological survival, like hunger and thirst.

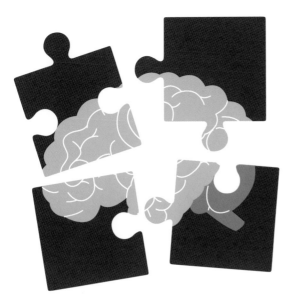

Brainstem: the very base of the brain, which performs many automatic functions necessary to life.

Bullying: the intentional harm of another, which involves an imbalance of power between the two.

Bystander effect: the tendency for people to fail to react to an emergency if others around them are ignoring it.

Causation: one thing makes another thing happen.

Cerebellum: covered by the cerebral cortex, this part of the brain keeps us balanced and upright.

Cerebral cortex: the outer part of the brain, which in humans is large and complex.

Change blindness: the tendency for an observer to not notice a change in a visual item or scenario.

Chunking: grouping information into "chunks" to make it easier to remember.

Circadian rhythm: your sleep and wake cycles.

Classical conditioning: pairing a stimulus that has a natural, automatic response with another stimulus over and over again until the second stimulus also triggers the automatic response.

Climate change: a long-term change in global temperature and weather patterns.

Cognitive dissonance: having thoughts or beliefs that are in conflict with behavior.

Cognitive psychology: the field within psychology that studies thinking, memory, perception, learning, and other brain functions.

Cognitive-behavioral principles: the idea that thoughts, feelings, and behaviors are interconnected and influence one another.

Cognitive-Behavioral Therapy: a type of evidence-based mental health treatment that focuses on the way unrealistic thoughts lead to upset feelings and problem behaviors.

Concussion: a brain injury resulting from a blow to the head.

Confirmation bias: a psychological tendency to seek out and believe information that supports what we already think.

Construct validity: how well a test or other tool measures what it's supposed to be measuring.

Control group: people or animals who are similar to sample groups, but who don't get the experimental treatment.

Controlled processes: step by step thoughts and actions that require attention and effort.

Cope: deal effectively with difficulty.

Correlation: two things tend to change together, but it's not clear which makes the other happen or if they are both changed by something else.

Cortisol hormone: a substance produced in the body, released in response to stress.

Crystallized intelligence: the knowledge, facts, and skills that we learn as we grow.

Cyberbullying: peer harassment online. It can be directed to the victim or involve indirect comments about them sent to others.

Data: evidence about whether a hypothesis seems to be correct or not.

Depression: when being down or sad lasts too long and interferes with daily life.

Depth perception: the visual ability to see in three dimensions, allowing a person to see drop-offs and judge distance.

E

Eating disorders: a number of psychological problems which lead to eating too much or too little.

Ecosystem: an interdependent system of organisms (animals, fish, plants, etc.) and the settings in which they live.

Empathy: the ability to put yourself in another person's position and feel for them.

Environment: the surroundings in which an animal, person, or plant lives. Environment often refers to the natural world but can also describe man-made habitats.

Ethical: an ethical experiment is one that is respectful of participants and protects them from harm.

Evidence-based: when several careful studies have been done by different researchers to show that a treatment works.

Experiment: a scientific procedure done to make a discovery or test a hypothesis.

Extrinsic motive: an urge to do something that comes from wanting to get a reward or praise or avoid punishment from other people.

F

False belief task: a task to show whether a child can see that another person does not have the same information that they have.

Fight or Flight: the reaction of our bodies to get ready to deal with danger by attacking (fight) or running away (flight).

Fixed mindset: the belief that one's abilities can't change.

Fluid intelligence: logical problem solving and reasoning.

Frontal lobe: the part of the brain responsible for thought, attention, problem solving, planning, and judgment.

Gender: society's interpretation of the roles males and females should play and the behaviors they should exhibit.

Gender identity: a person's feeling about whether they are a boy, a girl, or have aspects of both genders. Gender identity may or may not be the same as how the person appears to other people.

Gratitude: appreciative, thankful.

Grit: perseverance and passion for long-term goals.

Group think: the tendency for people in a group to share the same ideas, even to the point where creativity and different ways of thinking are discouraged.

Growth mindset: the belief that one can learn and improve abilities.

Hemisphere: a sphere divided into two parts. The brain is has two hemispheres.

Heuristics: mental short cuts that help with thinking.

Hormones: chemical messengers that travel through the bloodstream.

Hypothalamus: a part of the limbic system that communicates with the pituitary gland.

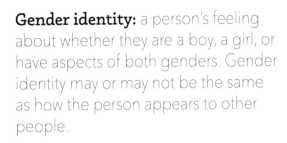

Hypothesis: a scientist's educated guess about the answer to a question.

Imagery Rehearsal Therapy: a method of developing a new end to your nightmare and rehearsing the new ending when you are relaxed during the day.

Implicit bias: an automatic, unintended reaction to another person based on their membership in a group that often results in treating them unfairly, even without awareness.

Impression management: the strong drive people have to act and look in ways they feel others will like.

Intelligence: the capacity to learn from experience, understand and control one's own thinking processes, and adapt to the surrounding environment.

Intrinsic motive: an urge to do something that results from a person's own feelings about that action.

Learned helplessness: the general belief that one has little or no control of the environment.

Limbic system: a set of brain structures concerned with emotion.

Longitudinal: when a study takes repeated measurements or observations over time.

Long-term memory: information that is stored for a long period of time, even years.

Mind: feelings, perceptions, thoughts, memories, and other actions that people cannot see.

Mind-body connection: the brain, via thoughts and feelings, influences the body and its functions. The health of the mind affects the health of the body.

Mindfulness: staying in the present moment with awareness and acceptance.

Modeling: learning through watching others and copying their behaviors.

Motivational contagion: when intrinsic motives are increased through observing others who are highly motivated.

Motor cortex: the part of the brain that controls voluntary movement.

Multiple intelligences: groups of abilities that extend the concept of intelligence to include more areas of functioning.

Nature versus nurture: the question of whether a behavior or mental experience is the result of biology, learning, or both.

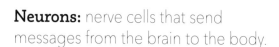

Neurons: nerve cells that send messages from the brain to the body.

Neuroplasticity: the capacity of the brain to form new brain pathways.

Nonverbal cues: indications of how a person is feeling that don't include language, such as facial expressions, gestures, and body language.

Object permanence: knowing an object still exists even when it is hidden.

Occipital lobe: a part of the brain that is important for vision.

Operant conditioning: a type of learning based upon what happens as a result of a behavior. When a behavior is rewarded it is more likely to be repeated.

Optimism: a tendency to expect good things to happen in the future.

Oxytocin: a hormone released by the pituitary gland.

Parietal lobe: a part of the brain that deals with senses and spatial awareness.

Peer pressure: the influence of others to conform to a group, which can lead to changes in behavior, values, or beliefs.

Perception: how your brain interprets information collected through senses.

Personal space: the distance from another person at which one feels comfortable.

Personality traits: a person's consistent patterns of behavior, ways of thinking, and feelings across different situations and time periods.

Pessimism: a tendency to have negative expectations for the future.

Pituitary gland: an endocrine gland that sits close to the hypothalamus and releases hormones.

Pollution: contamination with harmful or poisonous material.

Positive psychology: the scientific study of positive human functioning.

Preconscious information: information in the mind that is available to bring to awareness.

Prejudice: judging a person or people, often negatively, based on their appearance or group membership.

Primacy effect: the tendency for facts, impressions, or items that are presented first to be better learned or remembered than material presented later in the sequence. When it comes to other people, the first impression a person makes tends to have a strong impact on our opinions about them.

Priming: exposure to information that helps bring preconscious information to mind.

Pro-environmental behaviors: actions which help to sustain the environment (such as limiting energy use, avoiding waste, and recycling).

Psychological motives: motives to achieve happiness and good feelings.

Psychology: the science of behavior and the mind.

PTSD: Post-traumatic Stress Disorder. Persistent feelings of stress and anxiety after experiencing or witnessing a traumatic event.

R

Reaction time: the amount of time it takes to respond to something.

Reciprocal determinism: the idea that a person influences the environment and, in turn, is influenced by it.

Rehearsing: mentally reviewing information in short-term memory in order to transfer it to long-term memory.

Reliability: how consistently something leads to the same finding.

REM: the stage of sleep in which you dream. It is called Rapid Eye Movement because your eyes move quickly in different directions. Sleep stages 1 to 3 in which you generally do not dream are Non-REM.

Research Psychologist: a psychologist who uses the techniques of science to study questions about the mind and behavior.

Resilience: the ability to adapt well in the face of challenging life experiences.

Response efficacy: the degree to which people believe that what they do will lead to a specific result.

S

Sample group: the people (or animals) who are being studied. Psychologists try to include a diverse group of participants.

Sampling bias: the sample group does not match the characteristics of the bigger group it's meant to reflect.

Satisficing: accepting a good enough option.

Scientific Method: systematic observation, measurement, and experimentation, including making hypotheses, testing them, and modifying them as necessary.

Self-fulfilling prophecy: when beliefs about someone's personality traits result in treating them differently which leads them to act in ways that make those beliefs come true.

Self-motivation: the drive to follow through on one's own goals or intentions.

Self-talk: one's inner conversation.

Senses: sight, hearing, touch, taste, and smell. Information is collected through sensory organs (eyes, ears, skin and pressure sensors, taste buds, and nose) and sent to the brain.

Separation anxiety: fear when apart from an attachment figure.

Sex: an assignment of being male or female based upon biological factors.

Sexual harassment: unwanted or inappropriate sexual remarks, advances, or touching.

Sexual orientation: an identity based on who a person is attracted to.

Shaping: the process of teaching a behavior that an individual (animal or person) isn't currently doing. Behaviors that are increasingly close to the desired behavior are reinforced.

Short-term memory: information that is stored for less than a minute.

Social aggression: gossiping about someone or taking other actions to damage someone's social relationships or belonging to a group.

Social norms: behaviors that a person is expected to conform to in a particular group.

Social power: the ability of a person to get others to conform even when the others may not prefer to do so.

Social support: family and friends who help you feel cared for.

Stereotypes: expectations about preferences, beliefs, and behaviors of a group of people.

Stigma: a negative connotation associated with a particular quality, circumstance, or person, often resulting in shame.

Strange situation: a lab set up with a parent and a stranger coming and going from the room in order to observe attachment behaviors.

Stress: the feeling of being overwhelmed or unable to cope due to an event or circumstance.

Stroop effect: the observation that our ability to process familiar information slows down when interfering information doesn't match.

Survey: directly asking people about how they feel, what they think, or what they want.

Syllogism: a form of reasoning in which a conclusion is drawn based on two given statements.

Synesthesia: one sense automatically triggers a second one. For example, the person hears a sound and sees a color.

Temperament: consistent individual differences in mood and behavior seen from infancy.

Temporal lobe: a part of the brain important in language, hearing, memory, and emotion.

Theory of mind: recognizing that others have their own thoughts and feelings.

Transgender: a person whose sense of their own gender doesn't fit with the biological sex they were assigned at birth.

Verbal aggression: name calling, yelling, screaming or insulting someone in an effort to harm them.

Visual cliff: a test using a piece of equipment that has a drop-off, to see if a baby has developed depth perception.

Working memory: holding on to information in your head while you are also thinking about other information.

INDEX

A

Achievement motives, 143
ADHD (attention-deficit/
    hyperactivity disorder),
    185–186
Affiliation, 140–141, 143
Aggression, 183–184, 213
Agreeableness, 53
AI (artificial intelligence), 94
Ainsworth, Mary, 120
Allow the experience to be
    there (RAIN exercise), 155
Allport, Gordon, 52
Ambiguity, 220
American Psychological
    Association, 11, 154
Amygdala, 43
Analytical abilities, 90
Anderson, Craig, 215
Anger, 183–184
Angry thoughts, 136
Animals
circadian rhythms of, 166
research on learning using,
    78–79
as research participants, 21
research using rewards with, 82
Anxiety, 151, 179–180
Anxiety disorder, 181–183
Apophenia, 29
Applied behavior analysis
    (ABA), 187
Applied psychology, 14
Approach goals, 145
Aronson, Elliot, 213

Asch, Solomon, 193, 196
Attachment, 120–121
Attari, Shahzeen, 230
Attention
for controlled and automatic
    processes, 107
and memory, 97–99
and mental health, 185–187
and mindfulness, 155
in nature, 157
Attention-deficit/hyperactivity
    disorder (ADHD), 185–186
Attractiveness, 195
Authority figures, 198, 217–218
Autism spectrum disorder,
    187–188
Automatic processes, 107–109
Autonomic mimicry, 134
Availability heuristics, 110
Avoidance goals, 145
Avoidant, 121
Aykroyd, Dan, 188
Balance, ears and, 32

B

Bandura, Albert, 58, 65, 81,
    145, 214
Baoding balls, 156
Barnum, P. T., 52
Barnum & Bailey Circus, 52
Barnum effect, 52
Beck, Aaron, 172
Behavior
changing, with rewards, 77

defining, 8
in emergencies, 200
influenced by environment,
    228–229
predicted by personality traits
    or situations, 55
pro-environmental, 226–232
Biases, 206–207, 210
Big Bird (character), 52
"The big five" personality traits,
    50–52
Binet, Alfred, 84, 85
Biological motives, 137
Black people
implicit bias about, 209
stereotypes about, 208
Bobo doll experiment, 81
Body clocks, 164–165
Body smart, 89
Bowlby, John, 120
Bowles, Samuel, 144
Brain injuries, 45–46
Brain measurement
    technology, 39
Brains, 36–47
activity of, 38–40
as control tower, 101
hemispheres of, 40–41
and hormones, 44
interpretation of senses by,
    27–29
laughing and, 91
making assumptions based on
    experience, 29–30
parts of, 37, 42–43
safety for, 44–46

during sleep, 162–163

Brainstem, 37

Bullying, 215–217

Bushman, Brad, 215

Bystander effect, 200

Campos, Joseph, 120

Carlsmith, James, 113

Caso, Letizia, 133

Cattell, Raymond, 52

Causation, 18–19

Centers for Disease Control
    and Prevention (CDC), 165

Cerebellum, 37

Cerebral cortex, 37, 40

Chabris, Christopher, 98

Challenging your thoughts,
    137, 183

Chang, Yun, 157

Change blindness, 98

Child-rearing, 66

Choice (four C's of self-
    motivation), 145–146

Chunking, 99, 101

Cialdini, Robert, 13, 197, 231

Circadian rhythms, 164–165

Clark, Russell, 220

Classical conditioning, 74–77

Clayton, Susan, 10

Climate change, 229

Clouds, finding shapes in, 28

Cognitive-behavioral
    principles, 172–173

Cognitive-behavioral therapy,
    182

Cognitive dissonance, 113–114

Cognitive psychology, 91–94

Community (four C's of self-
    motivation), 145–146

Competence (four C's of self-
    motivation), 145–146

Competition, 145, 152

Computed tomography scan
    (CT scan), 39

Concussions, 45–46

Confirmation bias, 206–207

Conflict, 212–221

bullying, 215–217

between groups, 213–214

and helping, 219–220

between individual people,
    214–215

and social power, 217–219

Conscientiousness, 53

Consequences (four C's of self-
    motivation), 145–146

Construct validity, 53

Control, 172–173

Control group, 19

Controlled processes, 107–109

Coping, 112, 154–155

Correlation, 18–19

Cortisol hormones, 151

Creative abilities, 90, 93

Creative thinking, 186

Crum, Alia, 153

Crying

by babies, 117

composition of tears, 130

Crystallized intelligence, 85

CT scan (computed
    tomography scan), 39

Cuddling, 44

Cyberbullying, 217

Darley, John, 198

Data, 14

Decision making, 108–109

Deeprose, Catherine, 107

Darley, John, 200

Data, 16

Decision making, 110–111

Deeprose, Catherine, 109

Denmark, 177

Depression, 182–183

Depth perception, 119

Development, 116–125

and attachment, 120–121

newborns, 117–118

and personality, 60

and temperament, 121–122

of thinking, 122–124

visual development, 118–120

Differences in people,
    prejudice based on, 206

Discoveries, of psychologists,
    14

Distractions, 99

Draganich, Christina, 166

Dreaming, 161–162

Duckworth, Angela, 175

Duffy, Sean, 227

Dweck, Carol, 176, 177

Ears, and balance, 32

Eating disorders, 184–185

Ecosystem, 225
Ectomorphs, 51
Education, 11, 66
Einstein, Albert, 93
Ekman, Paul, 129
Elliot, Andrew, 144
Ellis, Albert, 172
Emergencies, 200, 220
Emotional signals, 135
Emotions, 128–137
and dreaming, 161
emotional signals, 135
and insights, 92
and limbic system, 43
negative emotions, 131
nonverbal cues to, 132–134
number of, 130
of other people, 134
and physical reactions, 131–132
and reactions to experiences,
    135–136
universality of, 129
Empathy, 123
Emperor's New Clothes, 219
Endomorphs, 51
Environment, 224–233
behavior influenced by,
    228–229
feelings of helplessness related
    to, 225–226
positive changes to help,
    226–227
research on messages related
    to, 13
and response efficacy, 229–230
social influence about saving,
    231–232
stress related to, 225

Erdal, Kristi, 166
Escher, M. C., 29
Ethical concerns, in research, 22
Evidence-based treatments, 182
Ewert, Alan, 157
Excitement, 135, 140
Exercise, 45
Expectations, 88, 166
Experience(s)
brains making assumptions
    based on, 29–30
causing stress, 150
emotions and reactions to,
    135–136
and intelligence, 85
and intelligence tests, 87
with people of other races, 210,
    213–214
and personality, 58–60
shared, 195
Experiments, 16
Expert opinions, 198
Extreme weather, 225
Extrinsic motives, 138
Extroversion, 53
Facial expressions, 129

Fads, 199
Failure, dealing with, 171
False belief task, 124
False memories, 103–104
Fear
and excitement, 135
learning and unlearning, 76
physical reaction to, 132

Feelings. See Emotions
Festinger, Leon, 113
Fight or flight response, 132,
    151
Finland, 177
First impressions, 193–194
Fixed mindset, 176–177
Fleeson, William, 54
Fluid intelligence, 85
fMRI (functional magnetic
    resonance imaging), 39
Forgas, Joseph, 182
Four C's of self-motivation,
    145–146
Freud, Sigmund, 51
Froh, Jeffrey, 178
Frontal lobe, 37, 42
Functional magnetic resonance
    imaging (fMRI), 39
Gaither, Sarah, 210

Gardner, Howard, 89
Geller, Scott, 1435
Gender, 62–71
and gender identity, 69–70
identification with, 64–65
sex and, 62
stereotypes about, 63, 65–69,
    207–208
Gender identity, 69–70
Gender pay gap, 69
Getting along, 196–197
Gibson, Eleanor, 119
Gilliam, Walter, 209
Goldstein, Noah, 13

Gordon, Peter, 91
Grades, 18
Graffiti, 228
Grandin, Temple, 188
Gratitude, 178
Griskevicius, Vladas, 13
Grit, 175
Group think, 213
Growth mindset, 176–177

Happiness Research Institute, 177
Harlow, Harry, 31
Haynes, Michelle, 69
Health, of brains, 44–46
Hearing, 32, 118
Heilman, Madeline, 68
Helping, 219–220
Helplessness
feelings of, 225–226
learned, 172
Hemispheres, of brains, 37, 40–41
Heuristics, 110
"Hijra," 70
Hiroto, Donald, 173
Hormones
cortisol hormones, 151
and neurons, 44
Hudson, William, 30
Humor, 91
Hurricane Katrina, 225
Hypothalamus, 44
Hypothesis, 16

Identical twins, 23, 58-59
Imagery rehearsal therapy, 166
Implicit bias, 209
Impression management, 198
Influence of others, 201
Information
brain filling in missing, 29–30
preconscious information, 111
tuning out of, 99–101
Insight, 94–95
Intelligence, 83–95
artificial intelligence, 94
and insight, 92–93
testing, 84–88
and thinking, 91–92
types of, 89–91
Intelligence quotient (IQ), 85–88
Interests, people with similar, 195
Intrinsic motives, 138–140
Investigate the feeling with kindness (RAIN exercise), 155
IQ (intelligence quotient), 85–88
Islam, and terrorism, 207

Jackson, Lenore, 88
"Jigsaw classroom," 213
Jobs, and gender, 68–69

Kahneman, Daniel, 111
Kanzi (bonobo), 92
Keizer, Kees, 228
Kellner, Robert, 164
Koko (gorilla), 92
Kremer, Kathleen, 10

Language, 91, 118
Latane, Bibb, 200
Laughter, 93, 136
Learned helplessness, 172
Learning, 74–83
classical conditioning, 74–77
modeling, 81–82
and motivation, 144
and movement, 187
operant conditioning, 77–79
rewards and punishments in, 80
Levin, Daniel, 99
Limbic system, 43
Litter, 228
Little Albert experiment, 75-76
Loftus, Elizabeth, 104
Logic smart, 89
Longitudinal studies, 19
Long-term memory, 100, 103
Lundstrom, Johan, 9
Lying, 133

Magnetic resonance imaging (MRI), 39
Maier, Steven, 172
Maine, 227
Manly, Jennifer, 11
Maric, Marija, 112
Markey, Patrick, 59
"Marshmallow Test," 20
Martin, Leonard, 134
Maslow, Abraham, 142
Math
fMRI of brains while working on, 39
and gender, 67
Memory, 96–105
and ADHD, 186
and attention, 97–99
and dreaming, 161
false memory, 103–104
long-term memory, 103
short-term memory, 99–101
working memory, 101–102
Mental health, 180–189
anger, 183–184
attention, 185–187
autism spectrum disorder, 187–188
eating disorders, 184–185
traumatic events, 185
worry and sadness, 181–183
Mesomorphs, 51
Milgram, Stanley, 217
Mind, 8
Mind-body connection, 151
Mindfulness, 155–156

Mind reading, 112
Miranda, Lin-Manuel, 143
Mischel, Walter, 20
Modeling, 81–82
Monkeys, research on, 31
Motivation, 138–147
achievement motives, 141
and affiliation, 140–141
biological motives, 139
and competition, 145
interactions between different, 143–144
and learning, 144
and needs, 142–143
psychological motives, 140
self-motivation, 145–146
Motivational contagion, 141
Motor cortex, 42
Movement
and learning, 187
and memory, 186
MRI (magnetic resonance imaging), 39
Multiple intelligences, 89
Murayama, Kuo, 144
Musicophilia, 43
Music smart, 89

National Football League (NFL), 86
National Spelling Bee champions, 175
Nature
research on connecting with, 10
stress and exposure to, 157–158

Nature smart, 89
Nature versus nurture, 21, 56–57
Nature videos, 157–158
Needs, 139, 142–143
Negative emotions, 131
Nervous system, 38
Neurons, 38, 44
Neuroplasticity, 38
Neuroticism, 53
Newborns, 117–118
Nichols, Tim, 9
Nightmares, 163–164
Nisbett, Richard, 55
Nolan, Jessica, 231
Non-identification (RAIN exercise), 155
Non-REM sleep stages, 162
Nonverbal cues, 132–134
Norway, 177

Object permanence, 123
Objects, thinking about, 122–123
Occipital lobe, 37, 42
Odbert, Henry S., 52
Openness to new experiences, 53
Operant conditioning, 77–79
Optimism, 173
Oscar the Grouch (character), 54
Other people
conflict between, 214–215
emotions of, 134
forming social groups with,

203-204. *See also*
Relationships
ideas about, in development, 123
need to connect to, 140-141
prejudices based on differences in, 206
Overgeneralizing, 112
Oxytocin, 44

Palena, Nicola, 133
Parietal lobe, 37, 42
Pavlov, Ivan, 74
Peer pressure, 196
Penn Resiliency Program, 174
People smart, 89
Perceptions, 29-30
Performance, 166
Personality, 50-61
and experiences, 58-60
and nature versus nurture, 56-57
personality traits, 50-54
and person's situation, 55
Personality traits, 50-54
Personal space, 43
Pessimism, 173
Petrified Forest, 197
Pet Rocks, 199
PET scan (positron emission tomography), 39
Pettigrew, Thomas, 210
Philpot, Richard, 220
Phone numbers, remembering, 99

Physical reactions, 131-132
Pi, remembering digits of, 100
Piaget, Jean, 122-123
Picture smart, 89
Piraha tribe, 90
Pituitary gland, 44
Playground, research on, 17-18
Plutchik, Robert, 130
Pollution, 225
Positive psychology, 170-179
cognitive-behavioral principles related to, 172-173
dealing with failure, 171
gratitude in, 178
perspectives in, 173-175
stick-to-itiveness in, 175-177
Positron emission tomography (PET scan), 39
Posttraumatic stress disorder (PTSD), 185, 225
Practical abilities, 90
Practicing, of controlled processes, 108
Preconscious information, 109
Preferred sides, 41
Prejudice, 205-206, 210
Primacy effect, 193-194
Priming, 109
Pro-environmental behaviors, 226-232
Proof, 16-23
Psychlab, 94
Psychological motives, 140
Psychologists, 9-14
Psychology, 8-15
PTSD (posttraumatic stress disorder), 185, 225

Punishments
in learning, 80
and motivation, 143-144

Questions, answering, 12-13

Race, 208-209
RAIN exercise, 155
Rapid eye movement (REM), 161
Reactions
to experiences, and emotions, 135-136
physical reactions, 131-132
Reaction time, 40
Reciprocal determinism, 58
Recognize the feeling (RAIN exercise), 155
Rehearse, 100
Relationships, 192-201
authority figures in, 198
building, 194-195
and emergencies, 200
first impressions, 193-194
and formation of social groups, 203-204
getting along, 196-197
importance of, 195
influencing others, 199
and teamwork, 198-199
Relaxation, 156-157
Reliability, 53

REM (rapid eye movement), 161
Research, 16–23
with babies, 117
checking design of, 19–20
correlation and causation in, 18–19
done by psychologists, 9–14
ethical concerns in, 22
that you can do, 17–18, 22
Research participants, 21
Research psychologists, 9, 13
Resilience, 174
Resistant, 121
Response efficacy, 229–230
Rewards, in learning, 80
Rosenthal, Robert, 88
Rozek, Christopher, 156
Rozenkrantz, Liron, 93

Sadness, 181–182
Salomon, Erika, 230
Sample, 18
Sample group, 19
Sampling bias, 19
Satisficing, 110
Savage-Rumbaugh, Sue, 92
Saver, Dustin, 186
Schacter, Stanley, 141
School psychologists, 9
Scientific method, 17
Securely attached, 121
Seeing, of babies, 118–120
Segal, Nancy, 57
Self-care, 157

Self-control, 20
Self-fulfilling prophecies, 207–208
Self-motivation, 145–146
Self smart, 89
Self-talk, 155, 171
Seligman, Martin, 171–173
Senses, 26–35
brains' interpretations of, 27–29
importance of hearing, 32
importance of touch, 31
and perceptions, 29–30
working together, 32–34
Separation anxiety, 120
Serpell, Robert, 85
Service animals, 79
Sex, 69–70. See also Gender
Sexual harassment, 214
Sexual orientation, 70
Shaping, 78
Shared experiences, 195
Sheldon, William, 51
Short-term memory, 99–101
Shutts, Kristen, 64
Sidedness, 41
Simon, Herbert, 110
Simon, Theodore, 86, 87
Simons, Daniel, 98, 99
16PF (16 Personality Factors Test), 52
Skinner, B. F., 21, 58, 78
"Skinner boxes," 78
Sleep, 160–167
body clocks, 164–166
brains during, 162–163
and dreaming, 161–162
lack of, 166

and nightmares, 163–164
Sleepwalking, 163
Smell
of babies, 117
research on, 9
taste and, 34
Social aggression, 214
Social efficiency, 204
Social groups
conflict between, 213–214
formation of, 203–204
Social influence, 231–232
Social norms, 202–211
biases, 206–207
fighting negative stereotypes, bias, and prejudice, 210
and formation of groups, 203–204
influencing behavior with, 231–232
prejudice, 205–206
and race, 208–209
and self-fulfilling prophecies, 207–208
stereotyping, 204–205
Social power, 217–219
Social support, 156
Sommers, Samuel, 210
Stages, of sleep, 162
Stanford-Binety test, 86
Stepper, Sabine, 134
Stereotypes, 204–205
about gender, 63, 66–69
fighting negative, 210
Sternberg, Robert, 90
Stick-to-itiveness, 175–177
Stigma, about mental health,

180
Strack, Fritz, 134
Straight, 70
Strange situation, 120
Stress, 150–159
anxiety vs., 151
coping with, 154–155
and exposure to nature,
    157–158
and mind-body connection,
    151
and mindfulness, 155–156
positive and negative affects of,
    152–154
related to environment, 225
and relaxation, 156–157
Stroop, J. Ridley, 108
Stroop effect, 108
Superstitions, 29
Survey, 18
Syllogism, 111
Synesthesia, 33

Taste, 34
Teamwork, 198–199
Temperament, 121–123
Temporal lobe, 37, 42
Terman, Lewis, 86
Terrorism, 207
Thanksgiving, 178
Theory of mind, 123
Thinking, 106–115
about stress, 152–153
and artificial intelligence, 94
controlled and automatic

processes, 107–109
creatively, and ADHD, 186
decision making, 110–111
development of, 122–124
errors in, 111–114
and intelligence, 91–92
in positive psychology, 172
and REM sleep, 161
Thinking traps, 111–113
Thomas, Danny, 46
Thoughts, challenging, 137,
    183
Thunberg, Greta, 229
Tip-of-the-tongue experiences,
    109
Touch, 31
Towels, getting people to
    reuse, 13
Toy design, 10
Transgender, 69–70
Traumatic events, 185
Triarchic theory of human
    intelligence, 90
Tuning out, of information,
    97–99
Tversky, Amos, 111
Twins, 21, 56–57
"Two spirited," 70

Underestimation of ability to
    cope, 112
Unhelpful thought, 137, 183

Verbal aggression, 214
Verges, Michelle, 227
Video games, 9, 59
Violence, exposure to, 59, 81,
    214, 215
Visual cliff, 119–120
Visual development, 118–120
Visual patterns, 27–28
Vygotsky, Lev, 12

Walk, Richard, 119
Walker, Matthew, 161
Watson, John, 58, 75
Wegner, Daniel, 154
Well-being, 172–173
White, Holly, 186
Witnesses
of bullying, 216
memories of, 104
Word, Larry, 220
Word smart, 89
Working memory, 101–102
Worry, 181–183

Yousafzai, Malala, 67
YouTube, 18

Jacqueline B. Toner, PhD, and Claire A. B. Freeland, PhD
are clinical psychologists in Baltimore, MD, with over thirty
years each in private practice working with children and
parents. They are the authors of several bestselling self-help
books for young people.

Visit jacquelinetoner.net, clairefreelandphd.com,
and @C_AB_Freeland on Twitter.

Magination Press is the children's book imprint of the American Psychological Association.
Through APA's publications, the association shares with the world mental health expertise and
psychological knowledge. Magination Press books reach young readers and their parents
and caregivers to make navigating life's challenges a little easier. It's the combined power of
psychology and literature that makes a Magination Press book special.
Visit maginationpress.org and @MaginationPress on Facebook, Twitter, Instagram, and Pinterest.